Teaching Junior Highers

Teaching Junior Highers

Lin Johnson

ACCENT BOOKS
Denver, Colorado

All Scripture quotations are from the King James Version.

ACCENT BOOKS

A division of Accent Publications, Inc.
12100 West Sixth Avenue
P.O. Box 15337
Denver, Colorado 80215

Printed in the United States of America

Library of Congress Catalog Card Number 86-70949

ISBN 0-89636-200-0

To all the junior highers
in Sunday school classes and youth
groups I have been privileged
to work with and to call my friends.
You have enriched my life in ways
too numerous to mention.

Contents

Contents

Preface

"Who are *you*?" said the Caterpillar.

. . . Alice replied, rather shyly, "I—I hardly know, sir, just at present—at least I know who I *was* when I got up this morning, but I think I must have changed several times since then."

"What do you mean by that?" said the Caterpillar sternly. "Explain yourself!"

"I can't explain *myself*, I'm afraid, sir," said Alice, "because I'm not myself, you see."

"I don't see," said the Caterpillar.

"I'm afraid I can't put it more clearly," Alice replied very politely, "for I can't understand it myself, to begin with; and being so many different sizes in a day is very confusing."

This quote from *Alice's Adventures in Wonderland* is an apt description of junior highers. They are confusing to themselves as well as to their parents and the adults who work with them. This confusion leads many adults to view them as frustrating problems to be solved and/or a species to be feared and dreaded.

But young teens also are terrific people—so terrific, in fact, that you may even come to consider them your favorite people, as I do. The major key that opens workers' attitudes to this latter perspective is an understanding of early adolescents and of how to teach them effectively. Hopefully, this book will be that key for you.

Lin Johnson

Some of the students' names have been changed to protect them.

PART ONE

Understanding Junior Highers

1 Welcome to Their World

Which of the following items best depicts a junior higher? Why?

- clock or watch at 7:00
- spaghetti dinner with tossed salad, garlic bread, and ice cream pie
- flower garden with several varieties of flowers in bloom
- traffic signal on yellow
- winding road with no end in sight
- waves lapping a rocky shore
- computer
- erupting volcano
- Halloween masks
- several football players tackling one another

As you perhaps have surmised already, there are no wrong answers to this question. Junior highers are at such a disparate and interesting age that all of the above descriptions can fit them. They have entered that mysterious world called adolescence.

ADOLESCENCE

Adolescence is a relatively new designation for this life stage. The widespread popular awareness of youth did not begin until after World War I. It was an outgrowth of three social changes in America: education laws which mandated that youngsters attend school until a certain age, child labor laws which prevented teenagers from working full time, and juvenile delinquency laws which separated teenagers from adults.

Before these changes in our society, adolescence did not exist, just as it is absent in many other cultures today. Children went directly into adulthood upon entering puberty.

CHILDHOOD	ADULTHOOD

Puberty

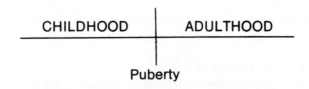

The sociological phenomenon that we have in American culture can be diagrammed like this:

CHILDHOOD	ADOLESCENCE	ADULTHOOD
Dependence	Transition ages 12-21/24	Independence

As people go on to graduate schools for longer periods of time and/or stay at home for more years, primarily due to economic factors, this transitional period labeled adolescence is lengthened. Some sociologists are now setting age thirty as the cutoff.

Regardless of the upper age limits which are set for adolescence, junior high is recognized as the beginning of this period. Young teens have become people under construction in a no-man's-land between children and adults.

Time of Change

Some of the major life changes take place during adolescence. For example, a teenager's reproductive system becomes active, he grows physically due to his adult build (barring width gains), he acquires the ability to think abstractly, he switches allegiance from parents to peers, he develops his own identity, his faith in God becomes very personal. Every aspect of his being is affected by change. These changes begin during the junior high years.

Time of Difficulty

All the changes that adolescents experience make this stage of life a difficult one. The difficulties are compounded by the fact that they are neither children nor adults. When I think back to my junior high years, I'm thankful I'll never have to repeat them! As a teenage boy commented, "It's hard to be a teenager because everybody seems to know what I need and want more than I do" (quoted by Carl A. Elder in *Youth and Values: Getting Self Together*, 1978, p. 31).

Time of Self-Definition

Teenagers are people in transition—no longer children but not quite adults. So they are wrestling with the question, Who am I? They are trying to develop their own identities, to become separate people from their parents.

Time of Independence

Closely related to their search for identity is the teenagers' drive for independence. Moving out of the total dependence of childhood, they are preparing to be independent adults. Usually they want more independence than they are ready for, however.

Time of Different Culture

Adolescents have become a subculture in our society when even commercial enterprises recognize the buying potential of teens. Each new teenage generation has its own music, dress, language, etc., creating a cultural gap between adolescents and adults.

Time of Sameness

Each new generation differs from the previous one, but some things never change, as the following quote, speaking of the youth of the author's time, indicates:

> All their mistakes are in the direction of doing things excessively and vehemently. They disobey Chilon's precept by overdoing everything; they love too much and hate too much, and the same with everything else. They think they know everything, and are always quite sure about it; this, in fact, is why they overdo everything.

These words easily could describe the present generation of teenagers. But they were written by Aristotle, a Greek philosopher, in the fourth century B.C. (*Rhetoric*, Book II, in *The Complete Works of Aristotle*, vol. 2, ed. by Jonathan Barnes, 1984, p. 2214).

CULTURAL INFLUENCES

In addition to being part of a subculture with its own characteristics, junior highers are greatly influenced by the adult culture around them. Some of the major influences from both sides are described in this section.

Philosophical Influences

Young teens have inherited self-centered thinking from society at large. The prevailing philosophy is *me first, me second,* and *me third.* Christopher Lasch has labeled it the culture of narcissism in a book by that title. As Lasch described the situation,

> To live for the moment is the prevailing passion—to live for yourself, not for your predecessors or posterity . . . .

> Narcissism appears realistically to represent the best way of coping with the tensions and anxieties of modern life, and the prevailing social conditions therefore tend to bring out narcissistic traits that are present, in varying degrees, in everyone. These conditions have also transformed the family, which in turn shapes the underlying structure of personality. A society that fears it has no future is not likely to give much attention to the needs of the next generation, and the ever-present sense of historical discontinuity—the blight of our society—falls with particularly devastating effect on the family. The modern parent's attempt to make children feel loved and wanted does not conceal an underlying coolness—the remoteness of those who have little to pass on to the next generation and who in any case give priority to their own right to self-fulfillment. The combination of emotional detachment with attempts to convince a child of his favored position in the family is a good prescription for a narcissistic personality structure (*The Culture of Narcissism*, 1979, pp. 5, 50).

In putting themselves first, teenagers tend to think in terms of what they can receive from a situation, rather than what they can contribute. Like many adults, they may say, "I don't get anything out of the church services," and label God and His church boring.

Adolescents with a me-istic attitude do not understand the words *no* and *wait*. They expect people to cater to their desires, an expectation often modeled by parents with the same attitude. They live for today; *now* is all that is important. The past is outdated, and the future is very uncertain, so all they have is the present.

Junior highers also have inherited a hedonistic philosophy: If it feels good, do it. Motivation is fueled by pleasure. Their lives are controlled more by feelings than by standards, including God's commands and principles given in the Bible. Teenagers have been conditioned to validate standards by experiences, instead of absolutes. Consequently, they need to experience Christ and Christianity in personal ways.

Closely related to this pleasure orientation is the relativism of society. Modern man—and adolescents—tend to live as though there were no absolutes. Everyone sets his own standards; one person's values are as good as another's.

Today's young teens also are part of a negativistic generation, primarily because they are living in a world of change and global problems. Adults have not been able to solve such crises as energy problems, starvation, terrorism, Communism, and the threat of nuclear war. Consequently, our young students live in a world full of questions without answers.

Science and Technology

In addition to the prevailing philosophies of our day, junior highers are influenced by rapid technological changes. Computers, for example, have changed our lives in countless ways, accelerating the transformation of our society from an industrial one to an informational one. They are reshaping education and fast becoming household necessities. Young teens will graduate from high school with computer literacy being considered one of the basics of a good education along with English and history.

In *Future Shock*, Alvin Toffler quoted statistics from Dr. Robert Hilliard of the Federal Communications Commission which involve today's young teens concerning the rapid pace of knowledge:

> At the rate at which knowledge is growing, by the time the child born today graduates from college, the amount of knowledge in the world will be four times as great. By the time that same child is fifty years old, it will be thirty-two times as great, and 97 percent of everything known in the world will have been learned since the time he was born (1970, p. 141).

Along with all that knowledge, what will your junior highers know about God and the life He wants them to live? Will they be able to integrate the two?

Advances in medical science have reduced diseases and

prolonged lives. Transplants and artificial organs, for instance, are becoming more common. But medical advances also have opened up a Pandora's box of ethical issues with which young teens will need to be prepared to grapple.

Issues they already are facing are the teaching of evolution as fact in the public school system and the resulting dehumanization of man. They need to know how God fits into those areas.

As a result of all the changes in technology and science, the past grows even more distant and the future becomes remote and uncertain, producing stress and lack of security. These can result in depression and even suicide for young teens.

Family Instability

Today's young teens probably do not have the same concept of family as you do.

> Most of us raised or were raised in a typical nuclear American family: Father was the breadwinner, mother took care of house and children, usually two. But today, there is no such thing as a typical family. And only a distinct minority (7 percent) of America's population fits the traditional family profile . . . .
>
> Today's family can be a single parent (male or female) with one or more children, a two-career couple with no children, a female breadwinner with child and househusband, or a blended family that consists of a previously married couple and a combination of children from those two previous marriages (John Naisbitt in *Megatrends*, 1984, p. 261).

By the next decade, half of all young teens will be from divorced and remarried homes, and stepfamilies will be the norm by the next century ("When 'Family' Will Have A New Definition." *U.S. News and World Report*, May 9, 1983, p. A4). Teenagers are the ones who suffer most from the divorce and remarriage of their parents. They need stability at home to counteract all of the changes happening in their physical, mental, emotional, and social development. Without this stability, they suffer from a lack of self-esteem, worth, and love. Young teens feel rejected by the parent who leaves and are cheated out of a normal adolescence since often they are expected to have more home responsibilities and help with younger children. If their parents remarry, they feel twice rejected. Teens from divorced homes usually become tougher on the outside to cover up the emotional hurts on the inside. They may blame themselves for the divorce and feel so guilty that suicide becomes the only viable option in their limited thinking.

Parent-Teen Relationships

The generation gap is highly overrated, especially for the younger teens. In a 1984 study of 8,000 church-related early adolescents, the number one-ranked value (out of twenty-four) was "happy family life"; their parents also ranked it number one (out of sixteen). The teens' fifth-ranked value was "make parents proud."

In spite of young teens' normal drive for independence, parents still remain the most important influence in their lives:

> We find that young adolescents do become, or want to be, independent of their parents. Though it is true that peers become more influential between the 5th and 9th grade, and that parents become less so, we also find that in no grade does the influence of peers outweigh the influence of parents. When asked where they would turn for help and guidance on a variety of topics, in every case, young adolescents seek out parents more than their peers. And as shown in the section on values, "To make my parents proud of me" is valued more than maintaining friendships (Search Institute, *Young Adolescents and Their Parents*, Summary of Findings, 1984, p. 44).

There is a tension, however, between the control parents want to exercise over their junior highers and the freedom the teens desire. So there will be clashes. But it is encouraging to know that young teens and parents highly value one another.

Sexual Ethics

Junior highers face far more pressures in the sexual realm than their parents did. They live in a society where the media uses sex to sell everything and glorifies it outside of marriage. The Biblical standard of waiting until marriage is a lost theme. On top of this pressure, their biological time clocks do not coincide with our culture's delay of marriage until at least after high school, in most instances.

Even though they are just entering puberty with its accompanying sexual drive, a significant portion of young teens have experimented with sexual intercourse. The Search Institute study, cited previously, discovered that twenty percent of early adolescents have done so (p. 14 of the report). Teen pregnancy, even among junior highers, is on the rise.

A somewhat related problem is the sexual abuse of teens. Although reliable figures are not available, "experts cite studies indicating that as many as 25 percent of the country's female population and 20 percent of the male population are sexually molested by the age of 16" (Randy Frame, "Child Abuse: The Church's Best Kept Secret?" *Christianity Today*, February 15, 1985, p. 33).

Substance Abuse

Alcoholism is a growing problem among adolescents. By the time they are in junior high, about eighty-five percent of them have drunk enough alcohol to get high at least once. Twenty-five percent have tried marijuana, and about five percent have experimented with other drugs. The figures for the church-related teens in the Search Institute study were only slightly lower.

Young teens are using drugs, including alcohol, for a variety of reasons. Some experiment out of curiosity, pleasure seeking, or peer pressure. Others do so to bolster a low self-esteem or to escape from problems or unhappy situations at home or school. Although drug abuse among teenagers is declining, drinking is increasing due in large part to widespread social acceptance; alcohol is very much a part of the American way of life. Also the media have strongly influenced young teens, who are imitators, to drink through associating beer with sports in commercials and portraying many television characters as social drinkers.

Suicide

Suicide is either the second or third leading cause of adolescent deaths, depending on what source you read. Regardless of the ranking, it has become an epidemic, increasing 300 percent in the last two decades for high school- and college-age youth. Junior highers and even younger children are attempting and succeeding at suicides at alarming rates.

Why do young teens want to kill themselves? The number one reason is a belief that they are not loved; they feel rejected by the important people in their lives—parents, peers, teachers. Problems at home or school, too high parental expectations, and divorced parents can plunge junior highers into a lasting depression that leads to suicide attempts.

Mass Media

Junior highers have been babysat, entertained, and mesmerized by the television set. They already have logged more hours watching it than they will spend in school through college, but most of what they watch contradicts and mocks Biblical values and standards. The same bill of fare permeates the movie, book, and magazine industries.

In the music realm, young teens' values and attitudes are being shaped by X-rated lyrics which glorify sex, perversion, violence, drugs, and the occult.

On top of these predominantly negative influences, advertising aimed at teens teaches them to be materialistic and covetous.

CHALLENGE TO TEACHERS

Because young teens face incredible pressures today, they need and want adults who will love them, listen to them, and introduce them to the God Who specializes in coping with impossible situations. One of those significant people can be you. The rest of this book will help you to understand them better and to work with them effectively. Are you ready?

QUICK REVIEW

1. Young teens are experiencing a number of difficult changes in their lives.

T F

2. Junior highers want to be more dependent upon adults than they were as juniors.

T F

3. Junior highers, like the adults around them, tend to put themselves first.

T F

4. Young teens generally are not influenced by pleasure-seeking, relativistic standards.

T F

5. Young teens have difficulty coping with changing family structures and divorce and remarriage of their parents.

T F

6. Parents are the most important influence in the lives of junior highers.

T F

7. Very few early adolescents have experimented with sexual intercourse.

T F

8. Suicide has reached epidemic proportions even among young teens.

T F

Answers:

1. T 2. F 3. T 4. F 5. T 6. T 7. F 8. T

2 Physical Development

As we observe the often mystifying physical developments that change children into adults, the "fearfully and wonderfully made" of Psalm 139:14 becomes awesome.

PUBERTY

The beginning of adolescence is usually said to be marked by puberty. This is defined as the physical changes that result in reproductive maturity. In our society the age is around 12, though it may vary one to several years either way. This physical change is sparked by a part of the brain called the hypothalamus, which—following instructions from ultramicroscopic genes—signals the pituitary gland to send out hormones. These hormones cause other glands, including the thyroid, the adrenal gland, and the gonads, to produce hormones that stimulate growth of the body and development of adult sexual characteristics (Kurt W. Fischer, Arlyne Lazerson, *Human Development*, 1984, p. 564).

As their sex organs mature, adolescents become capable of reproduction, with girls reaching this stage of development about one to two years before the boys. This maturity is accompanied by sexual drives which morally cannot be satisfied.

For the girls, puberty is marked by the onset of menstruation which probably will be very irregular for a year or two. Their breasts develop, body hair grows, and their hips widen.

The beginning of puberty is less easy to distinguish for boys, but ejaculations and pubic hair are generally recognized as the markers. During this time, testes enlarge gradually; then the penis lengthens. The boys may be embarrassed by erections at the most inopportune times. Due to the lengthening of their vocal cords, boys also experience voice changes. Squeaks and cracks happen frequently.

RAPID GROWTH SPURT

Early adolescence also is characterized by a rapid growth spurt, beginning sooner for the girls than the boys and at different times for everyone. We tend to view physical growth like the dotted line in the diagram below—steady and even until a person reaches adult height as a teenager. But in reality there are two major growth spurts, one during the first two years of life and the second during early adolescence as depicted by the solid line in the diagram.

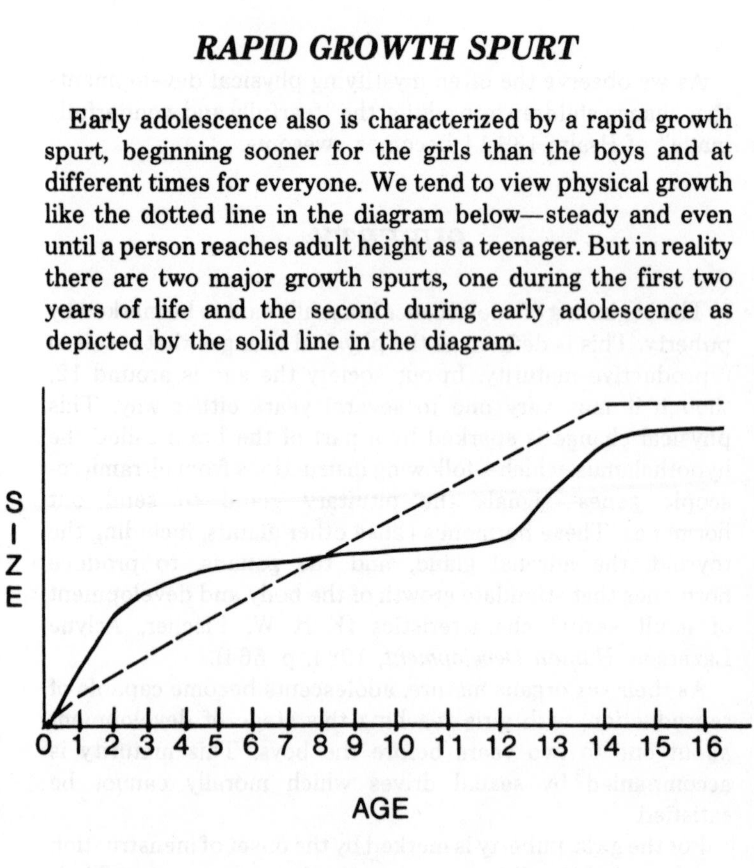

Dr. Perry Downs, Trinity Evangelical Divinity School, Deerfield, IL. Unpublished. Used with permission.

During this second growth spurt, young teens grow taller, heavier, and stronger. Physical growth is very irregular, however. The bones and muscles do not grow evenly nor at the same time. Early adolescents normally grow three to six inches in a year and gain twenty to thirty-five percent in weight. Girls often will develop poor posture trying to hide their towering height so they do not look so conspicuous in comparison with the boys and even other girls. I can still hear my mother nagging me to stand and sit up straight when I wanted to hide the fact that I was too tall.

The heart grows fifty percent larger, almost doubling in weight. Due to the resulting increase in blood flow, young teens have the greatest resistance to communicable diseases except for colds and respiratory problems. As glands develop and change, they produce complexion problems—perhaps the greatest curse of teens—which in turn cause feelings of inferiority and ugliness.

Since physical growth is irregular with large muscles developing before smaller ones and limbs, hands, and feet growing faster than the rest of the body, young teens tend to lack coordination. A boy may be five feet three inches with size ten feet, for example. Tall boys may be labeled basketball players but not be able to run down the court without stumbling. It isn't uncommon for teenagers to trip over the pattern in the tile floor and spill their beverages at the dinner table like young children, to their dismay and embarrassment.

ENORMOUS APPETITE

One of the results of such rapid growth is an enormous appetite. In addition to the fact that their stomachs are larger and can hold more food, young teens need more energy for growing. They become bottomless pits. When I was in junior high, I could outeat my father at any meal—to his astonishment—and then go back to the kitchen for a snack half an hour later. Now that I am an adult watching young teens eat, I am still amazed that the five foot, ninety pound girls in my class can eat two or three hamburgers plus everything else at a picnic and then eat another large meal two hours later. And those same girls are never overweight!

ENERGY AND FATIGUE

Another major result of the growth spurt is alternating periods of energy and fatigue. Sometimes young teens are bursting with energy and cannot sit still for two minutes. Other times they are so tired they cannot move even after ten to twelve hours of sleep. It is not unusual for these changes to take place within an hour or two of each other. I have watched my students go nonstop at a social for about an hour and then complain because they are tired. But within fifteen to thirty minutes they are active again and repeat the cycle.

Like babies, they sleep and eat a lot because growing so much takes large amounts of energy and can leave them drained. In spite of the fact that they are older, they need more sleep than they did when they were younger. They may appear to be lazy when actually their endurance is low.

PREOCCUPIED WITH APPEARANCE

All of these changes in their bodies make junior highers very conscious about how they look, especially in comparison with other young teens around them. They worry that they are abnormal, either growing too fast or too slowly, and are afraid of how they will turn out as high schoolers or adults. It is deadly to be either an early or a late bloomer; everyone wants to be on the same growth schedule as everyone else.

On the positive side, this new interest in their bodies usually results in improved grooming habits. The girls spend a lot of time in front of the mirror and experiment with cosmetics, often going overboard. The boys suddenly decide they should keep their hair combed and their shirts tucked in. Both take showers and wash their hair without having to be told several times.

SURVIVING THE CHANGES

Junior highers need adults who are sensitive to the physical changes they are experiencing and accepting of them just as they are. Refrain from teasing them, laughing at their awkwardness, or calling attention to physical traits. Instead, praise and compliment them for changes for which they are responsible, such as Biblical attitudes, mechanical skills, or cooking ability. Doing so will build their self-esteem.

Reassure young teens that the changes happening in their bodies and the differences in physical development among group members are normal. They are still in process and are not yet the finished products. They will grow or stop growing; they just need to give their bodies time. There is hope!

Instead of expecting junior highers to sit still for forty-five to sixty minutes—even though it is physically impossible for them to do so—plan to involve students in Sunday school. A variety of activities with opportunities to move around will help them to learn far better than a long lecture. (See Chapters 10 and 11 for method suggestions.)

Since boys and girls are not maturing at the same time, you may find it advantageous to separate the sexes for Sunday school. Both will feel more comfortable. Because boys are never sure if their voices will be normal when they speak or if they will sound more like a girl than themselves, they may be shy about speaking in class if there are girls in the same group. Teachers can get greater cooperation from their students, both boys and girls, in separate classes.

If there is enough space and teachers are available, it is even better to have four or six classes, separating the department by grade as well as sex since there can be big differences in maturity between seventh and ninth graders. If you can have only four classes, combine the eighth and ninth graders, rather than seventh and eighth graders.

For socials, emphasize group games that do not require physical skills rather than individual competitions which draw attention to awkwardness. Also plan quiet times to allow growing bodies to rest.

Teach your students that their bodies are the dwelling places of the Holy Spirit: "Know ye not that your body is the temple of the Holy Ghost which is in you, which ye have of God, and ye are not your own? For ye are bought with a price: therefore glorify God in your body, and in your spirit, which are God's" (1 Corinthians 6:19,20). As such, they should not use their bodies for sin or abuse them. Junior high age is not too young to teach Biblical standards for sexual conduct.

On the positive side, encourage students to take care of their bodies by getting plenty of sleep, eating a balanced diet instead of predominantly junk food, and developing good grooming habits. Be careful not to contradict your teaching by scheduling late events on school or Saturday nights or by planning meals and snacks without proper nutrition. You should model a proper attitude toward the body God gave you.

Finally, reassure students that God loves them no matter how they look. He is more interested in their bodies than they are since He designed both them and the changes they are experiencing, and He will help them through those changes.

QUICK REVIEW

1. Boys develop physically sooner than girls.
   T F
2. Junior highers have to cope with sexual drives.
   T F

3. Physical growth is steady and even for young teens.

T F

4. A young teen needs to eat and sleep more than adults.

T F

5. Junior highers frequently run out of energy.

T F

6. Awkwardness is a normal characteristic of young teens.

T F

7. Most junior highers do not care about how they look.

T F

8. A junior high student has no problem sitting still for an hour lecture.

T F

9. Group games for young teens should not involve individual skills.

T F

Answers:

1. F 2. T 3. F 4. T 5. T 6. T 7. F 8. F 9. T

3 *Mental Development*

"Why doesn't the government just make people work instead of paying them to stay home?"

"How do we know Christianity is true and the only way?"

"*Why* do you say Christians shouldn't go to movies? The Carlsons go, and Mr. Carlson is a trustee."

These tough questions are the kinds that junior highers start asking because of their mental development. Not only are they experiencing radical physical changes; but their thinking ability changes as well, primarily in the kind of thinking they are able to do.

FORMAL OPERATIONAL THOUGHT

Four major stages of cognitive or thinking development, as outlined by Swiss psychologist Jean Piaget, have come to be valued by most educators. The first three occur during childhood with the fourth, *formal operations*, generally happening around ages 12 to 15, although it begins with some children as early as 10. The term "formal" refers to the abilty to think about the *form* of statements and ideas (Inhelder and Piaget, *The Growth of Logical Thinking*, 1958, p. 573.)

Formal operational thinking marks the change from thinking in concrete, literal terms to abstract thinking. The person who has reached this stage of development can deal with ideas and concepts; he no longer is tied to concrete objects for understanding. He is more interested in ideas than facts and can begin to grapple with moral and ethical concepts, such as justice and love.

He recognizes that words can have both literal and suggestive meanings. Consequently, he can understand puns, irony and sarcasm; comprehend the meanings behind parables and allegories; and grasp literary devices like metaphors, similes, and personifications.

The formal operations stage also brings the ability to develop a hypothesis and reason if it is true or not. For example, if you said to a child who has not reached this stage of thought, "Suppose snow is blue," he could not think about the problem because snow is white, and he hits a mental barrier. But a junior higher in the formal operations stage can think of a number of possibilities and what might be the consequences. He can deal with all kinds of hypothetical situations and build theories.

He can think about thinking and therefore put himself in another person's shoes. As a result, he is able to empathize (but does not always do so) and understand how Bible characters might have felt in difficult situations.

Because formal operational thinking does not develop all at once, a class of junior highers will have students at various levels of thinking ability. Most seventh graders still are primarily concrete thinkers; many ninth graders are capable of abstract thought.

INDEPENDENT THINKING

As a result of this new thinking ability, junior highers begin to think independently of parents, teachers, and other adults. They question everyone and everything, including their faith in Christ and Christianity in general since for the first time in their lives they have the ability to reason and question like this.

The whole process of working out for themselves what they believe can lead to conflicts with teachers as well as parents. In fact, some may appear to be agnostics instead of the believers you thought they were. Instead of squelching their questions with the response, "Just believe what I tell you," it is important to help adolescents work through their doubts and questions. Let them know it is okay to question; Christianity can stand up to even the most difficult questions.

DESIRE FOR REASONS

Another result of this new kind of thinking is a demand for reasons for doing something. "Because I said so" is no longer sufficient. A junior higher wants a specific reason. Consequently, he may become or appear to be very critical, constantly asking "Why?" He also may appear to be a know-it-all with an answer or alternative, as well as a question, for everything asked of him.

ARGUMENTATIVE

Closely allied with a desire for reasons is the fact that junior highers like to argue and debate. Formal operational thinking helps them to gather facts and make a case. Often they will argue for the sake of argument, a tendency which quickly can frustrate teachers.

EGOCENTRISM

Because of their new ability to think in different ways, junior highers perceive themselves as the center of the world, just as infants and young children do. It is not the same as egotistical pride but rather an inability to separate their own concerns about themselves and the changes that are taking place in their bodies from the interests of other people. Consequently, they assume everyone else is interested in them in the same ways and to the same extent they are interested in themselves.

One of the major results of this egocentrism is self-consciousness. Young teens think other people are far more aware of them and are watching them more than those people really are.

CONCERN FOR THE FUTURE

Past and future time perspectives are greater for junior highers than for children. To a primary child, three months seem like an eternity. But eighth-graders are beginning to think years ahead and are planning their futures, primarily in relation to careers.

In the light of the possibility of global nuclear war, some junior highers are asking, "Will there even be a future?" After drawing a doubtful conclusion, increasing numbers are opting for alternatives to planning for the future, such as alcohol and drug addiction and suicide.

SELF-IDENTITY

Although the search for self-identity is primarily centered in the senior high and college years, it begins in junior high. With all the changes taking place in his body, thinking ability, and emotions, an adolescent has every right to ask, "Who am I?"

He may feel totally worthless, especially in comparison with others. Physical changes can make him feel ugly while late development of the cognitive stage four can make him feel dumb. His critical attitude may turn inward, causing him to put himself down with such expressions as "I can't do anything right." This inferiority may develop into the belief that nobody cares about him or would miss him if he died.

While every aspect of his world is changing, a teenager faces the monumental task of integrating his strengths, weaknesses, goals, desires, and dreams for the future. In this effort to discover who he is and who he will be, a junior higher subconsciously will try on many personalities. One day he may be friendly and helpful, the next day, mean and antagonistic. At the beginning of the Sunday school period, he may be an extrovert but switch to an introvert by the time the dismissal bell rings. He may experiment with being the teacher's pet, the class cutup, a chameleon with no opinions of his own, a charmer, a fighter. Each time he tries on a new personality, he observes the way others react and repeats or discards the behavior accordingly. Eventually he will emerge from this process with a personality that is uniquely him.

During this process of identity development, it is important for teachers and parents to help junior highers cope with feelings of inferiority by encouraging them to become good at something. Dr. James Dobson, a noted Christian psychologist, calls this method of coping *compensation* and declares that it is the most effective way of coping (*Hide and Seek*, rev. ed., 1974, pp. 79-84).

As a teacher, you can help your students discover their strengths and develop them. A junior higher may have artistic talent; mechanical ability; a hobby, such as coin collecting; cooking expertise; sports ability; or any of a hundred other strengths. As you compliment Sue on a new dress she sewed herself and ask Gary to make a poster to illustrate a lesson truth and invite Sam to help you repair your car, you affirm their worth, making them feel loved and important.

Also, it is essential that teachers model God's unconditional acceptance by accepting each student as he is, including his limitations. Showing favoritism toward some students confirms the others' inferiority and worthlessness. As David expressed in Psalm 139:13-18, everyone is unique and special to God.

IMAGINATION

Junior highers have a very active imagination. They rarely turn it off, certainly not for Sunday school. At the most inopportune times, they pop out with unexpected and unrelated remarks and questions. For example, in the midst of a serious Bible discussion, one of my junior high girls asked, "Why does your ankle bone stick out like that?" After explaining that it is original equipment, I picked up the discussion where it had been interrupted and continued on.

LACK OF TACT

One does not have to work with junior highers very long to discover they say exactly what they think. If they do not like your dress or tie, they will tell you. If they think you are a hypocrite, they will let you know. If a student does something considered to be dumb in class, someone will be sure the rest of the group is aware of the blunder. If someone's nose is large or his teeth stick out, one of his peers will label him with a nickname which calls attention to that fact.

One thing young teens have never been accused of is tactfulness. As one adult described them, "The only problem with junior high kids is, they don't have filters between their minds and their mouths" (quoted by Dave McCasland in *From Swamp to Solid Ground*, 1980, p. 27).

SURVIVING THE CHANGES

With their new kind of thinking ability, junior highers need to be challenged to use it by thinking for themselves rather than being spoon-fed through weekly lectures. Guide them to learn God's truths for themselves through such involvement methods as role play, inductive Bible study, and questions.

(See Chapter 10 for details.)

When students question you and Christianity, give them answers and reasons. Don't be afraid to say, "I don't know, but I'll find out," instead of blundering through an answer. That response is much better than making one up and will increase respect rather than decrease it. As someone cautioned, "Be careful of speaking to the edge of your knowledge; you might fall off" (quoted by Elmer L. Towns in *Successful Biblical Youth Work*, 1973, p. 82).

Because they can reason and question in new ways, junior highers no longer are satisfied with lists of do's and don'ts in relation to Christianity. They need to know *why* we do or do not do certain things. Therefore, it is important to teach Biblical principles and standards, rather than dogmatically telling them what to do. Including "Children, obey your parents in the Lord: for this is right" (Ephesians 6:1) in the list of principles will prevent conflicts with parental teaching.

When students express doubts about their faith, do not judge or criticize them. Instead, help them to find answers in the Bible to work through those doubts. Doubts which are not resolved can turn into skepticism later.

Finally, be prepared at all times. Junior highers have very active minds as well as bodies. As Dave McCasland warns: "If you don't have anything planned, they do. A junior high girl is seldom at a loss for words, and a junior high boy seldom goes anywhere with empty pockets. Junior highs don't like to be bored, and most of the time, they carry their own alternatives with them. If you come up short in the planning department, they'll be happy to pick up the slack" (*From Swamp to Solid Ground*, 1980, p. 48).

QUICK REVIEW

1. Many junior highers are able to begin dealing with abstract concepts like justice and love.

T F

2. Junior highers are willing to be told what to do without questioning.

T F

3. Young teens will argue with you even if they do not disagree with you.

T F

4. One of the best ways to help junior highers cope with inferiority problems is to help them become good at one thing.

T F

5. Junior highers are careful about what they say so they will not hurt anybody.

T F

6. A good teaching method for use with young teens is lecture.

T F

7. A teacher should never say, "I don't know."

T F

Answers:

1. T 2. F 3. T 4. T 5. F 6. F 7. F

4 Emotional Development

Do you remember your first roller coaster ride with all of those frighteningly high peaks and sudden death drops within seconds of one another? (Or the first coaster you refused to ride because of those ups and downs?)

The roller-coaster moods of junior highers move from mountaintop highs to valley lows very quickly. Along with changes in their physical bodies and mental abilities, they are experiencing emotional upheavals, primarily due to glandular development. Some of those upheavals are accompanied by thrills and fears similar to the ones you felt on that first roller coaster ride.

YO-YO MOODS

Young teens' emotions are very unpredictable. They can fluctuate from one extreme to the other and all points in between in a short period of time. Tom, for example, may be joyful when he comes to class but switch to a sullen mood ten minutes later. Or Sue will cooperate one week and disrupt class the next Sunday. Like a yo-yo, a young teen consistently is up and down emotionally.

Sometimes a young teen's emotions may explode all over, unintentionally hurting people with the outburst. At other times, he may try to hide his feelings. Often he has difficulty talking about how he feels, even when he does not hide those emotions well.

Moodiness and depression frequently characterize one end

of these mood swings. However, they normally do not last long since the yo-yo of emotions also goes up to more pleasant feelings.

These changeable moods affect whole groups of young teens as well as individuals. One Sunday everyone in class may participate in the Bible study activities, causing you to rejoice. But the next week they all may sit defiantly in their chairs and dare you to teach them anything, motivating you to resign from contact with junior highers for life.

To many adults, these unpredictable extremes of emotions resemble schizophrenia. But for a young teen, they are normal.

INTENSITY

To a young teen, every experience appears king-size at one extreme or the other; there seems to be no middle ground. The emotions he experiences are extremely intense, often out of proportion for the situation.

When a junior higher is sad, he is totally depressed. In fact, the depression may seem so great that he considers or even attempts suicide because he lacks a mature perspective of the situation. When a junior high girl has a crush on her youth sponsor, she is more in love than anyone else has ever been.

This intensity of emotions may lead to angry outbursts over insignificant events or words. For instance, a teen may stomp out of class if he is not asked to be a buzz group leader when he thought he should have that position. A young teen can respond in blind rage for seemingly no reason at all. Then his anger can subside just as quickly.

LACK OF CONTROL

These intense, fluctuating emotions are difficult for junior highers to control. With all of the changes happening in their feelings, they do not understand the emotions, much less know what to do with them.

For example, a young teen may burst out giggling for no reason and then not be able to stop. One of the most vivid memories of my own junior high years is frequent periods of uncontrollable laughter without even knowing why I started laughing. This type of outburst often is infectious, causing a whole class to giggle and thus stopping the Bible study for a few minutes. A wise teacher pauses until the laughter subsides and then picks up at the point it began without making a fuss over the interruption.

LACK OF SELF-ESTEEM

Two typical junior high emotions are feelings of inferiority and insecurity. Because of all the changes taking place in his body, a teenager becomes very self-conscious. He often thinks nobody understands him—especially his parents. He goes through periods of feeling unliked by the whole world—including his best friend—and totally worthless.

Lack of understanding about the physical and mental changes brought on by puberty leads to those feelings of inferiority. In comparing himself to others, a junior higher feels he is not as good or as worthwhile as they are. To cover up these feelings, he may develop a loud, overbearing manner or cockiness. He may withdraw into a shell or become the class boss. Or he may feign a bored, sophisticated attitude which dares anyone to teach or help him.

To identify how your students feel about themselves, ask them to complete the following statements, in writing:

Complete this sentence ten times:
I am . . .

Most of the time I ______ myself.

FEARS

A junior higher experiences fears which may seem silly to the adults who know him. Most of them are imaginary but still very real to him.

Many of these fears are closely linked to the physical changes in his body. In comparing his looks with other young teens at various stages of growth and development, he may fear that he is physically abnormal. This fear leads to the fear of being socially unacceptable, especially if he is awkward and klutzy.

The fear of failure—of saying or doing the wrong thing—may lead a teen to give up without trying. When Jane was a seventh grader, she refused to participate in our class discussions even when she knew the answers or had opinions on a subject. Her mother clued me in on her fear of giving the wrong responses, so I did not press her. Two years later she had overcome that fear enough to actively participate in class. (I like to think that my personal interest, encouragement, and prayers helped.)

SURVIVING THE CHANGES

With daily lives characterized by intense, roller coaster feelings, junior highers need adults with consistent emotional stability. As you model control of your own emotions, you offer hope that the uncontrollable extremes will pass or can be conquered.

When individuals or the whole class are expressing unpleasant emotions, such as sullenness or defiance, be patient. Since their moods change quickly, you can expect more agreeable behavior soon. Much of the moodiness can be overlooked due to the fact that it is normal behavior.

Along with patience, flexibility and understanding will help you cope with such unpredictable and fluctuating feelings. If you do not expect adult responses, you will not be disappointed. Such reactions as overreacting, getting upset, criticizing, or publicly embarrassing teens quickly alienate them.

Love and acceptance of young teens as they are now—not as you wish they were—will help to build their self-esteem. (See "God and Self-Esteem.") Since teenagers spell love T-I-M-E, it is important to spend time with them outside of class—getting acquainted, doing things together, listening, being available. (See Chapter 12 for more details.)

Assure junior highers that emotions are not sinful, but they are responsible for the actions that result from those feelings. For example, Paul teaches in Ephesians 4:26-32 that anger is normal and okay: "Be ye angry" (verse 26a). But he also teaches that we should not hang onto that anger, letting it fester into bitterness and grudges: "Be ye angry, and sin not: let not the sun go down upon your wrath: neither give place to the devil. . . . Let all bitterness, and wrath, and anger, and clamour, and evil speaking, be put away from you, with all malice: and be ye kind one to another, tenderhearted, forgiving one another, even as God for Christ's sake hath forgiven you" (verses 26, 27, 31, 32).

Also assure young teens that faith is not built on feelings but on believing what God says in His Word, regardless of how we feel. John wrote his first epistle so his readers would *know* they have eternal life, not so they would *feel* they have salvation: "These things have I written unto you that believe on the name of the Son of God; that ye may know that ye have eternal life" (1 John 5:13).

In the midst of unpredictable and changing emotions, junior highers need to be reminded that God is unchanging. He is always the same; He is always available; He always can be counted on; He never fails.

Since young teens are highly emotional beings, it is easy to manipulate them into spiritual decisions by strong emotional appeals. However, those kinds of decisions usually last only as long as the emotion does—which is not long. It is better to avoid such tactics and encourage actions based on obedience to God and His Word, not on guilt or an emotional high.

God and Self-Esteem

God regards me as unique and special.

"For thou hast possessed my reins: thou hast covered me in my mother's womb. I will praise thee; for I am fearfully and wonderfully made: marvellous are thy works; and that my soul knoweth right well. My substance was not hid from thee, when I was made in secret, and curiously wrought in the lowest parts of the earth. Thine eyes did see my substance, yet being unperfect; and in thy book all my members were written, which in continuance were fashioned, when as yet there was none of them. How precious also are thy thoughts unto me, O God! how great is the sum of them! If I should count them, they are more in number than the sand: when I awake, I am still with thee" (Psalm 139:13-18).

God accepts me unconditionally.

"But God commendeth his love toward us, in that, while we were yet sinners, Christ died for us" (Romans 5:8).

God is not concerned with outward appearances.

"For the Lord seeth not as man seeth; for man looketh on the outward appearance, but the Lord looketh on the heart" (1 Samuel 16:7).

God has different values than man does.

"For that which is highly esteemed among men is abomination in the sight of God" (Luke 16:15).

QUICK REVIEW

1. Junior highers often express a variety of emotions within a short period of time.

T F

2. Junior highers are able to control their emotions fairly well.

T F

3. A young teen frequently feels misunderstood and worthless to others.

T F

4. In order to cure bad moods, a junior higher should be disciplined for them.

T F

5. Unpleasant emotions like anger are sinful.

T F

6. It is important to help junior highers base their faith on objective truth, not on feelings.

T F

Answers:

1. T 2. F 3. T 4. F 5. F 6. T

5 Social Development

A mother of one of the junior high girls in my Sunday school class stopped me after the church service. She wanted to talk to me about her daughter feeling shunned by the other two girls. It was a typical junior high problem. Only a few months before, that daughter had caused one of the other girls to feel the same way when she and the third girl were buddies.

Working through this type of social squabble is part of the maturing process for young teens. Along with physical, mental, and emotional changes is a corresponding shift in social relationships.

DRIVE FOR INDEPENDENCE

One of the major changes in the social realm for young teens is breaking away from their families and establishing a separate identity. They no longer are content to be known only as Mr. and Mrs. Brown's son or daughter; rather, they want to be recognized as their own persons who make their own decisions. Psychological growth has enabled them to realize that they are separate from their parents and they can think, see, and feel differently.

As a result of this breaking away, junior highers tend to be very critical of their parents and label them as old-fashioned. They may be embarrassed to be seen in public with them, and consequently avoid them as much as possible. Most young teens, for example, will part company with their families immediately upon arriving at church and join them only when called to go home.

This drive for independence is painful for parents who want to continue to maintain control. Various degrees of rebellious attitudes and actions emerge, usually in proportion to the amount of control parents are exerting. This rebellion against authority in an attempt to be independent carries over into other areas, including school and church.

In spite of the fact that junior highers desire to be grown-up, they often vacillate between acting as independent adults and reverting to dependent children, not quite ready for the responsibilities of independence. Consequently, they are very unpredictable!

PEER GROUP

The bridge between the security of dependence on parents and the freedom of independence is the peer group. It also is the dominant characteristic of a young teen's social life. As an extension of the junior-age gangs, junior high peer groups continue to be comprised of the same sex.

A strong desire to be accepted by a group influences junior highers to do almost anything. Whatever fashions the group is wearing, he wears. Whatever slang the group uses, he uses. Whatever the group likes, he likes. Whatever the group does, he does.

To be different is to commit social suicide. Consequently, it is difficult—if not impossible—for a junior higher to stand alone for the Lord and His standards when the group is not interested in or is acting in a manner contrary to the Bible. As Wayne Rice states, "If a choice must be made between friends and faith, they will choose their friends nearly every time. Faith can come later . . . . Having friends is the most important thing now" (*Junior High Ministry*, 1978, p. 70).

Even though the desire to belong and conform to the group is strong, some young teens alienate their friends by their behavior. Linda, for instance, wanted very much to be accepted by the rest of the Sunday school class, but her periodic obnoxious attitude and nosiness drove away her friends.

On the surface, this drive for conformity and lack of individual identity seems to contradict the junior higher's desire for independence and his own identity. However, the peer group actually functions as an aid to independence. It fosters social development by providing a wide variety of experiences in interacting with people and deepening interpersonal relationships. The group helps young teens to develop loyalties beyond their family units and helps them to adjust to more adult roles. There is the emotional security of acceptance and support in a peer group where other people affirm by their presence that that person is worthwhile.

The peer group of a Sunday school class or youth group can provide positive conformity as young teens support and encourage one another to live the Christian life. If Sunday school is a place where everyone is accepted and loved, each member will belong to at least one group.

HERO WORSHIPER

Although being accepted by a group of peers is important to junior highers, they still admire and imitate adults. This hero worship spills over from the junior age. They still idolize sports heroes, television and movie stars, and rock musicians, as well as ordinary adults who befriend them. This hero worship may even go as far as pasting an actress's picture on the front page of her Bible as one of my students did.

SELF-CONSCIOUSNESS

With all the upheavals in their bodies, emotions, minds, and social status, it is no wonder that junior highers can be very self-conscious. Without a healthy self-esteem to give them confidence and opportunities to practice social skills, they act out the uncertainty inside them.

For some young teens this self-consciousness is so strong that they become social introverts. For example, Jane who refused to participate in class, hung around the edge of the group during activities the first year she was in my class because she was afraid of saying or doing the wrong thing. Consequently, she chose to do nothing and was a social introvert.

BEGINNING INTEREST IN OPPOSITE SEX

Self-consciousness is seen most clearly and frequently in boy-girl relationships. Girls are beginning to take an interest in the boys but are not always open about it, certainly not to them. Most of the boys, however, are a year or two behind the girls in this interest since their physical maturity begins later.

With seventh and eighth graders, this disparity in interest in the opposite sex and reluctance to admit any interest frequently produces a tension thick enough to cut when boys and girls are in the same Sunday school class. It is almost comical to watch how the boys try to avoid sitting next to the girls and vice versa. Unfortunately, the tension decreases learning.

ACTION-ORIENTATION

Junior highers possess an enormous eagerness and enthusiasm for action. Unlike the more sophisticated high schoolers, they are ready to do anything. That "anything" may range from class participation to planning socials, or from group service projects for the Lord to mischief or trouble, depending on how their enthusiasm is channeled.

This characteristic makes teaching young teens a joy. I never have had a class that did not respond to suggestions for projects and any kind of participation in class. They have been eager to do from the word *go*.

SURVIVING THE CHANGES

Since junior highers desire to be grown-up, teachers need to treat them as such, remembering that they are not adults. When appropriate, let class members make decisions and take on responsibilities, i.e., planning a class social.

It is vital that you accept everyone who is in your class and not play favorites. Be friends with and show a personal interest in each student. Sunday school should be one group where everyone feels comfortable and knows he belongs and is loved. Make a special effort to include students who may be rejected by the rest of the group, seeking to discover why and doing what you can to alleviate the situation.

As a group, plan and participate in outreach and service activities for the Lord. It is not so difficult to practice Christianity when a whole group is doing the same thing. Teach and encourage friendship evangelism to help your young teens testify to their friends about the Lord without the fear of social ostracism. *Out of the Salt-Shaker & into the World* by Rebecca Manley Pippert (InterVarsity Press) is an excellent resource for this. Also encourage your students to seek out Christians at school for mutual support.

One of the by-products of peer groups is cliques. They can become so strong that it is an exercise in futility to try to break them up. Instead, provide opportunities for group members to interact with one another and participate together in class. It helps to form small groups randomly or around cliques without separating everyone from all his close friends.

This tendency to form cliques of teens of the same sex, plus their self-conscious reluctance to act naturally in the presence of the opposite sex are valid reasons for emphasizing the importance of having separate classes for boys and girls in the junior high department. If group size or lack of a second teacher is an obstacle to doing so, begin praying for and seeking more students or a teacher. Three faithful attenders are not too few for a class; and if they enjoy Sunday school, they will invite their friends, thus increasing the class size.

Since young teens are going to imitate adults they admire, a junior higher's teacher ought to be a prime candidate for his admiration and emulation. Be an example worthy of imitation even as Paul expressed in 1 Corinthians 11:1, "Be ye followers [imitators] of me, even as I also am of Christ."

Finally, capitalize on young teens' eagerness for action. Instead of lecturing, use involvement methods to help them to grasp Bible truth for themselves. (See Chapters 10 and 11.) Also plan—with their assistance—class socials and service projects. Do not let them use the excuse, "There's nothing to do," to justify channeling their energy into mischievous acts.

QUICK REVIEW

1. One major junior high task is to begin to establish themselves as separate people from their parents.
T F

2. Young teens' behavior is quite predictable.
T F

3. Peer pressure is always unhealthy.
T F

4. The peer group is a major influence in a junior higher's life.
T F

5. Junior highers are interested only in their peers, not in adults.

T F

6. Young teens are ready for action.

T F

7. A wise teacher can use peer group influence to help his students grow spiritually.

T F

8. Junior high workers should try to break up cliques.

T F

Answers:

1. T 2. F 3. F 4. T 5. F 6. T 7. T 8. F

6 Moral Development

"Knowing Jesus is great, but church is boring!"

"My parents tell me to obey God's Word, but they don't practice what they preach."

"I used to believe the Bible because my Sunday school teacher told me I should, but now I'm not so sure."

"I know I said I was saved in third grade and was baptized a year later, but sometimes I wonder if I'm *really* saved."

Remarks like these sound negative and seem like steps backwards in faith to many youth workers and parents. However, when you really think about them, you can see that they actually illustrate junior highers' growth toward more mature faith.

IDEALISM

One of the key words describing young teens' moral development is *idealism*. They want to be committed to something and make their lives count, to feel important. For both Christians and unbelievers, that desire can be channeled into following Christ. Many missionaries, in fact, dedicated themselves to serve the Lord in that way when they were in junior high.

An outgrowth of this idealism is a desire to serve the Lord. They readily respond to a variety of service projects, but their interest tends to be short-term. Sometimes, however, they have the wrong motives for serving. The girls may volunteer to work in the nursery, not only because they like children and want to do something for the Lord, but also to escape from church services they consider boring. The boys may offer to help with the sound system so they, too, can avoid sitting in church services as well as developing technical skills and using them for the Lord.

Another outgrowth of their idealism is a desire to know how to practice the truth they study although they probably need guidance in discovering ways to do so. They are more interested in knowing how the Bible relates to their immediate problems of pressure to cheat, loneliness, temptation to experiment with drugs or sex, etc., than in being able to recite a lot of facts.

In their search for a source of commitment, junior highers—ever imitators—scrutinize adults for consistent role models to follow. They are quick to detect hypocrites and to vocalize criticism of them in the church and home.

DOUBTS

A second key word for young teens' moral development is *doubts*. This characteristic is closely tied to their drive for independence and their beginning ability to think in new ways.

As children, their faith tended to be a hand-me-down from their parents or other respected adults, such as Sunday school teachers or club leaders. They believed primarily because they were told to do so. But now they begin to question those beliefs about faith in God, the church, the Bible, etc. They frequently question, "How do you *know* that's true?"

Contrary to what many adults perceive, questioning beliefs does not equal heresy or unbelief. As an old saying put it,

He who has never doubted
has never really believed.

It is healthy for a young teen to question and to think through what he believes in order for those beliefs to become internalized and not something to be discarded when independent from parents.

I would much rather have students who keep putting me on the spot with their doubts and questions than those who sit quietly, absorbing everything I say without thinking about it. Tina, for example, has had a question almost every week since she entered my class. Many of them I cannot answer because the Bible does not give us definitive answers in those areas. But I am excited that she is thinking and is not afraid to ask her questions. The type of teens who never doubt and question are prime candidates for cult groups.

DEVELOPMENT OF VALUE SYSTEM

Junior highers are developing a keen sense of right and wrong, resulting in strong conviction of sin. Although they are sensitive to disobeying God, often they are powerless to break a sinful habit without clear teaching on how to do so and the encouragement of adults whom they admire and peers who also are trying to follow the Lord. Rachel frequently talks with me about temptations she is facing and what to do about them. I can tell from her comments in class that certain Bible studies are helping her to overcome sinful habits which she really wants to have victory over. One-on-one counseling and prayer also have helped her to grow spiritually in these areas.

In keeping with their drive for independence, young teens are beginning to develop value systems that belong to them, not just to their parents. Unfortunately, their values frequently are influenced more by friends, the media, lack of stable families, and situation ethics than by the absolutes and principles God gave us in the Bible. Therefore, it is important for you to build relationships with your students and to share your values with them both verbally and by example as well as teaching God's standards and their applications to twentieth-century teenagers.

SPIRITUAL DECISIONS

Closely related to their idealism is the fact that junior highers often make solid spiritual decisions. Once they work through their doubts, Christianity becomes very personal. Although the literature on peak ages for Christian conversions does not always agree, it is recognized that ages twelve and thirteen are a high point for individuals to believe on Christ for salvation from sin.

One caution is in order here. Young teens' decisions can be strictly emotional. They are very susceptible to emotional appeals and can be pressured into almost any kind of decision with subtle or overt plays on their emotions. For example, it is fairly easy to pressure a whole group of junior highers to rededicate their lives to the Lord or to volunteer for missionary service by making them feel guilty apart from the Holy Spirit's conviction.

LESS INTEREST IN FORMAL STUDY

Most junior highers have "advanced" beyond the interest they had as juniors in completing their Sunday school lessons, memorizing the weekly verses, etc. Part of maturing is the temporary lack of interest in formal study.

However, young teens are capable of understanding much more of the Bible and will participate in class and even study on their own *if* such participation and study are interesting to them and they have good reasons to do so. For example, most will no longer memorize the weekly verse because the teacher expects them to—unless their parents also require it, and very few do. But they will memorize verses if they understand the personal value of doing so and know how to use the truth of those verses in their daily struggles to live for the Lord.

SURVIVING THE CHANGES

Even though the idealism and doubts of junior high age teens can be threatening to the adults who work with them, they need not be.

As young teens express their doubts and ask questions about God and their faith in Him, don't be shocked or condemn them. Instead, let them know that doubting is a natural process of growing, and it is okay to ask questions. When Jesus was twelve, His earthly parents "found him in the temple, sitting in the midst of the doctors [teachers], both hearing them, and asking them questions" (Luke 2:46). Encourage your students to follow His example and ask questions in and out of class.

Give your students Biblical answers, and help them work through the doubts. (See "Helping Students Work Through Doubts.") Reassure them that God still loves and accepts them even when they doubt Him. Jesus did not condemn John the Baptist when he expressed his doubts about Jesus' Messiahship (Matthew 11:2-6). Instead, He reminded John about the evidences with which he was already familiar. Even some of Jesus' twelve disciples doubted Him (Matthew 28:17), but they went on to be strong leaders in the church. There is hope!

Be prepared to meet your students' criticism of others. Help them to understand that God does not expect us as Christians to be perfect while we live here on earth; but He does expect us to keep striving toward Christlikeness and to be honest enough to admit when we've failed, ask for forgiveness, and go on. When fellow Christians seem to be hypocritical in what they say or do, it may help the students to improve their attitudes if they can see Christ in what we do and say.

You can help junior highers to channel their commitment into serving the Lord by planning short-term service projects with them. For instance, they could run errands for shut-ins on a couple of Saturdays, but don't expect them to commit every

Helping Students Work Through Doubts

"1. Give advice from experience not expertise." Share yourself and how you worked through your own doubts in the past.

"2. Ask more questions than you answer." Stimulate your students' thinking.

"3. Be free and give freedom." Allow your students the freedom to doubt.

"4. Love, don't lecture the person who has failed."

"5. Share faith, not formulas."

"6. Be a doubter." Admit your own doubts. Continue to question yourself.

Trent Butler, "To Doubt Is to Learn," *Youth Leadership*, April-June, 1985, pp. 20-21.

weekend for six months to this service.

Capitalize on young teens' interest in practical truth and action by leading them to discover ways to apply the principles of God's Word which they study in class. (See Chapter 9.) To offset their decreasing interest in formal study, make class sessions interesting and fun through using a variety of teaching methods. (See Chapters 10 and 11.) Junior highers are not a captive audience for lectures!

Since young teens readily respond to appeals for commitment and other spiritual decisons, be cautious about how you make such appeals. Let the Holy Spirit work instead of pressuring for decisions or playing on emotions. When God convicts, the decision will be a lasting one, not a temporary one.

QUICK REVIEW

1. Junior highers are idealistic.

T F

2. Young teens are eager volunteers to serve the Lord.

T F

3. Young teens continue to believe because parents and teachers tell them to.

T F

4. Junior highers have sensitive consciences even though they do not always listen to them.

T F

5. It is harder to motivate junior highers to do their Sunday school lessons than when they were juniors.

T F

6. It is important for teachers not to let their students know they have sinned.

T F

7. Young teens should not be allowed to express doubts or to question the Bible.

T F

Answers:

1. T 2. T 3. F 4. T 5. T 6. F 7. F

PART TWO

Teaching Junior Highers

7 You, the Teacher

Who is the most memorable teacher in your life? He or she may be a Sunday school, elementary, high school, or college teacher. Regardless of who this one may be, spend a few minutes thinking about that person. Why do you remember him or her as outstanding? What character traits and actions do you recall? Did that teacher influence you in a positive or negative way?

Teachers are important people in our lives. Their influence for good or bad is powerful, especially in Sunday school. For example, my junior Sunday school teacher is the most memorable in my life. She was interested in me as an individual and treated me as an important person even though I was just a shy kid. She cared enough about me to invite my whole family to dinner at her house. Most of all, she believed God would use me in great ways to serve Him. (She was convinced I would be a foreign missionary, but God never led in that direction.) As a result of her love and interest, I came to know the Lord personally as my Savior.

My junior high teacher had no memorable qualities either positively or negatively. In fact, I don't even remember if that person was a man or a woman! My senior high teacher was the catalyst for my dropping out of Sunday school and church for a couple of years because his class was boring, useless, and a waste of time—at least in my teenage opinion.

You can be the teacher junior highers remember in a positive way. This chapter focuses on a number of factors which help to shape an effective teacher for the Lord.

GIFT OF TEACHING

Although all Christians are to be teachers (Colossians 3:16; 2 Timothy 2:2), some are given the gift of teaching. Romans 12 tells us that each member of the body of Christ has been given at least one special gift to be used in the work for God done by the church, the body of Christ, and we should be diligent in using those gifts for God's glory. One such gift is teaching (verse 7). What is this gift of teaching and how can you know if you have it?

Definition

The gift of teaching is the supernatural ability to explain clearly and apply effectively the truth of God's Word. Like the other gifts, it is given by the Holy Spirit at salvation according to His sovereign will, not our desire. God gives it to believers so they in turn can help to build up the body of Christ. (See 1 Corinthians 12:1-11.)

This gift is not the same as natural talent, even though it may have some basis in natural ability. It is a spiritual gift. If the Spirit has not gifted the person who is teaching, he or she will never be a totally effective teacher and will not see the spiritual results that a gifted teacher will.

Discovery

There are a number of ways to discover or confirm if you have the gift of teaching. One of the most important ways is *to pray*. Ask the God Who gives the gifts to show you if He has given you this one or not.

Another equally important step is *to teach*. It is impossible to know if you have the gift of teaching without actually teaching. Volunteer to teach a class for at least a quarter since it takes time to see results. Also try working with different age groups. Some people are more effective with some ages than with others. For example, when I was only substituting, I was convinced I did not have this gift. But when I agreed to take a class for at least half a year, God made it clear that I do have the gift of teaching. When I worked with children, I was a total disaster. But when I concentrated on teenagers and adults, especially junior highers, the Lord confirmed the fact that He has given me this gift.

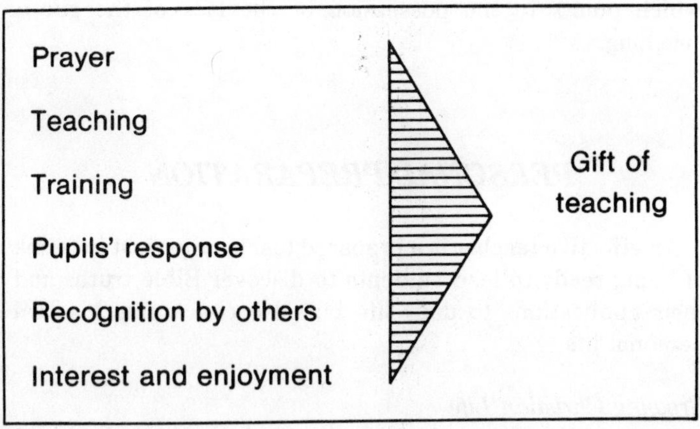

Another aid to discovering the gift of teaching is *training*. You may never know if you have the gift if you do not know how to exercise it. Teacher training classes, conventions, seminars, and reading books like this one all contribute to the ability to use the gift effectively.

Look for student *response*. Those who have the gift will see results in the lives of their students. Pupils will enjoy being in class and studying the Bible together as well as spending time with their teacher. They will be growing spiritually as they are encouraged and guided in applying the truths of the Bible to their everyday lives. (The fact that spiritual growth and building relationships takes time is an incentive to teach a class for more than a few weeks in order to discover if you have the gift of teaching.)

A fifth indication of possession of this gift is *recognition by others*. Besides the positive response of your students, other people who observe the class in session and your abilities will recognize that God has gifted you to teach His Word. Personal *interest* is another indication. Do you enjoy teaching, or is it pure agony? God wants us to take pleasure in serving Him, not to do so out of duty or guilt.

It is a combination of all of these factors, not just one or two, which points to the possession or the lack of the gift of teaching.

PERSONAL PREPARATION

An effective teacher is a prepared teacher, not just in terms of being ready to lead students to discover Bible truths and their applications to daily life but also concerning his own personal life.

Growing Christian Life

Several disciplines which produce spiritual growth should be part of your daily lifestyle. They are basic but very important. First, you must be a person who spends time with the Lord in personal Bible study and prayer. A teacher cannot live off secondhand truth garnered from sermons and books and quicky prayers said just before falling asleep. Prayer and firsthand Bible study need to be top priorities.

An outgrowth of that discipline should be obedience to God which leads to modeling the truth of His Word. First Peter 5:2,3 applies to Sunday school teachers as well as elders: "Feed the flock of God which is among you, taking the oversight thereof, not by constraint, but willingly; not for filthy lucre, but of a ready mind; neither as being lords over God's heritage, but being ensamples to the flock."

Knowledge of the Bible

Effective teachers are students of God's Word. Although you are not expected to know everything the Bible teaches, you should not be ignorant of the Bible, either. Attending Bible studies and formal classes, reading commentaries and Bible study books, and enrolling in correspondence courses all help to increase your knowledge of Biblical truths. These should not take the place of reading the Bible, however.

Development of Teaching Skills

Effective teachers not only are growing in their spiritual lives and knowledge of the Bible, but they are developing their God-given gift of teaching. Through training classes, seminars, and reading, you can increase your understanding of junior highers, learn new methods to use, and become a better communicator of God's Word. If you are a teacher, be the best you can be. (See Romans 12:3-8.)

Discipline

Effectiveness and self-discipline walk hand in hand. Effective teachers know how to order their schedules and priorities to be well-prepared to teach and to build relationships with students. You cannot wait until Saturday night to prepare lesson plans and have contact with class members only during Sunday school if you want to do your best for the Lord.

RELATIONSHIP WITH STUDENTS

In order to have a positive impact on junior highers, you need to take time to build relationships with them. There are four basic tools for building the kinds of relationships which cause students to respect and listen to you as you guide them in obeying God's Word.

Love

When people think of the most memorable teacher in their lives, they almost always name actions which are evidences of love. Teenagers especially remember ways love is expressed to them. They are drawn like magnets to adults who do more than talk about love but demonstrate it in relation to them. Consequently, we need to love our junior highers when they goof off in class, when they cut one another down, even when they walk away from the Lord. We must love them the way they are now, not the way we want them to be. And we must love them genuinely; junior highers can detect hypocritical actions every time.

This quality is so important in our Christian lives that Paul

13 and the Sunday School Teacher

1. Though I speak with words on my students' level of understanding and have not love, I am become as grating chalk or a yelling parent.

2. And though I have the gift of teaching and understand the whole Bible and creative methods; and though I am able to relate Scripture to my pupils' daily lives, and have not love, I am nothing.

3. And though I plan class socials, and though I visit each student's home, and have not love, it profits me nothing.

4. Love is patient with students who are slow, and kind to those who irritate me; love is not envious of other teachers' large classes; love does not boast of my perfect attendance, is not proud of the good ideas I have.

5. Does not shout at misbehaving students, is not selfish with my classroom and equipment, does not get upset when the opening assembly runs too long, lives a pure life as an example;

6. Does not gloat over sin in other teachers' lives, but is happy when they and my students do right;

7. Keeps on going when teaching becomes a chore, has faith in God's teaching through me, has confidence in my

wrote to the Corinthians that any abilities and gifts we have (like the gift of teaching) and any sacrificial acts we perform (like having an all-nighter with our students) are useless without love. He then described how true love acts (1 Corinthians 13). See "13 and the Sunday School Teacher," a paraphrase of that passage for teachers. As you read it, evaluate how well your love measures up.

students' abilities, endures the combining of classes at the last minute when a teacher is absent.

8. Love can be counted on at all times; but whether there be audiovisuals, they shall fail; whether there be exciting stories, they shall cease; whether there be learning centers, they shall vanish away.

9. For my students know in part, and I teach in part.

10. But when Christ comes, then my partial teaching will be done away.

11. When I was a new teacher, I lectured constantly, I did not understand the learning process, I thought my students came to study eagerly; but when I became a more experienced teacher, I put away ineffective methods.

12. For now I see my students' facades but then as they really are; now I know them only a little; but then will I know them even as the Lord knows me.

13. And now abides faith in God's working in my pupils' lives, hope for their growth as Christians, love for them as they are—these three. But the greatest of these is love.

This paraphrase by the author first appeared in *Key to Christian Education*, (Spring 1980).

Listen

Junior highers are surrounded by adults who talk at them and tell them what to do but rarely take time to listen to them. You can—and should—be the rare exception. Listen to what they mean as well as what they say, keeping in mind the old saying:

> ***I know that you believe you understand what you think I said, but I am not sure you realize that what you heard is not what I meant!***

Listen to the nonverbal clues as well as to the verbal. Observe his body language, expressions, and actions. What do they tell you about his feelings? Are they contradicting his words?

How you listen is just as important as taking the time to do so. Give the student your full attention, looking him in the eyes. Learn to be nonjudgmental and shockproof to what you hear. Teenagers like to tell adults things that will shock them just to see how they react before trusting them with the real problem. For example, Vicki announced that she did not believe in God anymore. But her real problem was the fact that she failed a test she did not study for, and God did not miraculously give her all the answers when she prayed for help.

Be a Friend

Junior highers are very relationship-oriented and value friendships with adults who show personal interest in them, especially outside formal settings like a Sunday school class. Studies have revealed that a teacher will double the effectiveness of his or her teaching by building relationships with students outside class, even apart from making any changes in the way he teaches during the class time. The closer the personal relationships, the greater the impact you will have on your students.

One of my joys of teaching junior highers is the friendships that have developed. At church socials they frequently seek me out for company. After graduating into the senior high department, they stop by my classroom to chat for a few minutes on Sunday mornings. Many of them are still good friends now that they are adults.

Affirm

As often as possible, affirm your students. Express appreciation for their presence and help, compliment them on new achievements or faithful attendance, be positive in responding to their contributions in class. Such affirmation builds their self-worth and demonstrates to students that you care about them as individuals.

The bottom line in teaching is the relationships you build with your students. Ten years from now they will not remember much of what you said to them. But they will remember the kind of person you were. Will your junior highers remember you as someone who loved them, who took time for them, who considered them to be important?

You teach a little bit by what you say.
You teach most by what you are.

The most powerful part of a lesson is the teacher behind it.

—Henrietta Mears

Doan, Eleanor L., compiler. *431 Quotes from the Notes of Henrietta C. Mears*, 1970, pp. 36, 46.

QUICK REVIEW

1. A teacher needs to have the gift of teaching in order to be most effective.
T F

2. The gift of teaching is the same as natural ability to work with people and teach them.
T F

3. If a person desires to be a teacher, he probably has the gift of teaching.
T F

4. Someone with the gift of teaching does not need training.
T F

5. Effective teachers discipline themselves to study and obey God's Word and to make teaching a top priority in their schedules.
T F

6. Teachers impact their students more by their relationships with them than by their formal teaching times in Sunday school.
T F

7. Teachers need to have an abundance of love for their students regardless of how they act.
T F

Answers:

1. T 2. F 3. F 4. F 5. T 6. T 7. T

8 *Principles of Teaching and Learning*

Eight junior high girls dressed in their Sunday best sprawled around the classroom floor. They built objects with Tinker-toys, glued pictures and words onto a large sheet of paper, and drew stick figures on poster board, talking all the time. The teacher sat on the floor and observed, occasionally asking and answering questions. When Ann walked by to collect the records, she was convinced those girls could not possibly be learning the Bible. After all, students are supposed to sit in chairs and listen to the teacher when they come to Sunday school.

Across the hall, seven junior high boys in dress shirts and ties fidgeted in two straight rows facing the teacher. The only one who talked was the teacher, and he told the group what the Bible passage said. As Ann picked up the record packet outside the door, she felt reassured that at least one junior high class was learning.

Was Ann right? Were the boys learning and the girls goofing off? As you read this chapter, compare your present ideas with the following definition and principles of the teaching/learning process.

DEFINITION

Contrary to Ann's perception, teaching is not just telling, although that may be part of the process. Consider these definitions:

Teaching is providing for and encouraging effective learning.

Learning is growth or change in information, attitudes, and/or behavior.

In other words, teaching is guiding students to make firsthand discoveries of what God's Word says and means and how to apply those truths to daily living. The teacher becomes a resource person and a guide instead of a dispenser of all truth. He or she creates the kind of environment in which students can discover and learn. Learning occurs when pupils practice those truths they have found in the Bible, resulting ultimately in changes of behavior. The student gets into the Bible, and the Bible gets into the student:

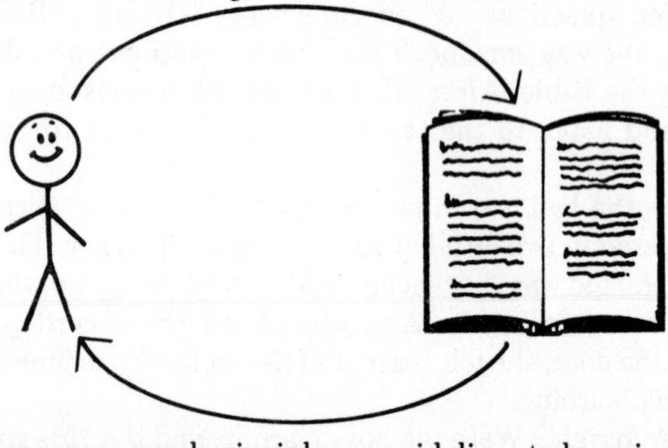

There are several principles or guidelines to keep in mind in order to help junior highers learn or grow. They are explained below. How to translate these principles into a teaching session is the subject of the next three chapters.

PRINCIPLE NO. 1
Expose students directly to the Bible as the final authority

We live in a society with very few standards and even fewer

absolutes. Whatever people feel like doing is okay as long as they do not break the law and get caught. It seems like everyone is a law unto himself with no outside authority to dictate what is right and what is wrong. In the midst of this relativism, part of a teacher's responsibility is to teach teens that the Bible is the final authority for beliefs and practices.

To do so effectively, you must guide them to learn for themselves what God's Word tells us to do, instead of merely telling them what God's Word says. One of the biggest dangers of lecturing to junior highers is the fact that they end up feeling accountable only to the teacher, not to God Himself—if they feel accountable at all.

One of your goals as a teacher should be to help your students know how to study the Bible for themselves and to find answers to their problems in God's Word without always having to rely on another source for information and guidance. (I am not implying that people, including teachers, and other books are not helpful. But the final authority for decisions and actions is the Bible.)

PRINCIPLE NO. 2
Relate the Bible to students' needs and experiences

The Bible is not a dull, dusty book written centuries ago with no relevance for modern junior highers. On the contrary, it is surprisingly up-to-date and contains a lot of guidance for the problems with which they are dealing. It is your job as a teacher to help your students intersect its teaching with their lifestyles. The following essay, "The Unheard Cry," highlights the importance of doing so.

The majority of people in the world today are silently crying, "DON'T YOU SEE I NEED HELP?" In every class there are those who have problems. A teacher in public elementary school related recently that there are more and more home-related problems even among the very young, as the ratio of broken homes continues to rise. Teenagers face perplexity, confusion and often acute problems.

Can a Sunday school teacher be satisfied with merely "teaching the lesson"? Teaching must be person-centered. A teacher must know the members of his class intimately and teach them in the light of their backgrounds, their interests and their needs. Jesus did. His teaching approach to doubting Thomas was different from the approach He used with vacillating Peter. His teaching to the sorrowing disciples was different from His method with the money changers in the temple.

The lesson from the Bible must be taught—this is correct. The Bible has the answers—this is true. But the teacher's job is to show how the Bible has the answers to an individual student's life with his background, his interests, and his particular needs.

The following testimony of a senior high school teacher should cause every earnest Christian teacher to pause and examine his own teaching: "I have taught in high school for ten years. During that time I have given assignments, among others, to a murderer, an evangelist, a pugilist, a thief, and an imbecile.

"The murderer was a quiet little boy who sat on the front seat and regarded me with pale blue eyes; the evangelist, easily the most popular boy in the school, had the lead in the junior play; the pugilist lounged by the window and let loose at intervals a raucous laugh that startled even the geraniums; the thief was a gay-hearted Lothario with a song on his lips; and the imbecile, a soft-eyed little animal seeking the shadows.

"The murderer awaits death in the state penitentiary; the evangelist has lain a year now in the village churchyard; the pugilist lost an eye in a brawl in Hong Kong; the thief, by standing on tiptoe, can see the window of my room from the county jail; and the once gentle-eyed little moron beats his head against a padded wall in the state asylum.

"All of these pupils once sat in my room, sat and looked at me gravely across worn brown desks. I must have been a great help to those pupils—I taught them the rhyming scheme of the Elizabethan sonnet and how to diagram a complex sentence!"

You may have the attention of your class Sunday after Sunday, but have ignored their silent cries for help in their lives that day and that week. Is God's Word relevant to today's people in today's complex world? If you know it is, make it relevant to the needs of your pupils.

"The Unheard Cry" appeared in *Success* Magazine, Accent Publications.

In order to relate the Bible to students' lives, you must know your junior highers personally and keep abreast of their needs. Knowledge of general characteristics of young teens, as described in Part One is a beginning. Chapter 12 outlines specific ways to become acquainted with the individuals in your class.

PRINCIPLE NO. 3
Learning begins with interest

Like adults, junior highers generally do not respond well to subjects and situations in which they have no interest and no outside motivation. Since Sunday school falls into the category of voluntary participation, even if parents make their teens attend, it is vital to arouse curiosity in students and gain their interest at the beginning of the hour. Otherwise, their bodies may be present, but their minds are checked out to other interests. How to hook students' attention is described in Chapter 9.

PRINCIPLE NO. 4
Learning is directly proportional to involvement

Learning is not a passive study. Unfortunately, many

Sunday school teachers treat it as such and expect their junior highers to sit still and soak in all the facts they dole out. As someone has said, "If telling were the same as teaching, we'd all be so smart we could hardly stand it." While telling must be an important part of teaching, "smartness" comes with understanding, and understanding is strengthened by doing—involvement. As an old proverb says,

I hear and I forget,
I see and I remember,
I do and I understand.

I heard a workshop leader describe the need for involving students in firsthand discovery of Bible truths by labeling the opposite situation as evangelical dumptruck teaching. All week long, he said, teachers get gems from their own Bible study and the teacher's manual. Then they put all these gems into a dumptruck, roll into Sunday school, and dump them all on the students. And the kids say, "Whoopeedo," and walk away unchanged.

When students are involved in discovering for themselves, they have ownership of the truths of God's Word. Then they will recognize their accountability for practicing these truths and will follow through. As a result, learning occurs.

PRINCIPLE NO. 5
Learning equals changed lives

Learning is more than the acquisition of Biblical facts. Rather, it is being transformed by those truths. When learning takes place, there are changes in information, attitudes, and actions.

Before Jesus Christ ascended into Heaven, He left His followers instructions which have been labeled the Great Commission: "All power [authority] is given unto me in heaven and in earth. Go ye therefore, and teach all nations, baptizing them in the name of the Father, and of the Son, and of the Holy Ghost: teaching them to observe all things whatsoever I have commanded you: and, lo, I am with you alway, even unto the end of the world" (Matthew 28:18-20).

The emphasis in the Greek is not on going but on making disciples. Part of the process of discipleship is teaching people to observe, or obey, everything He has commanded. In a church setting, *learning is obedience to God's Word which requires a change in lifestyle from the thinking and actions dictated by the old nature.* The more a person really learns the truths of the Bible, the more he or she thinks and acts like Christ. Throughout this process, Christ is present and helping people to change.

PRINCIPLE NO. 6
Learning results from identification

Much of what students learn—and consequently do—comes from observing people, including teachers. Therefore, it is imperative that you model the truths you teach. As Christ said, "The disciple [a student] is not above his master [teacher]: but everyone that is perfect [after he has fully learned what he has been taught] shall be as his master" (Luke 6:40).

Whether you realize it or not, you are reproducing your life into the lives of your students. When they leave your class, they will leave with some of you—positively, negatively, or both. In some respects, it is a scary responsibility. But it is also a wonderful privilege for you to model Christlikeness and know others are following Him as a result.

What are your students learning from your life?

PRINCIPLE NO. 7
Learning should be enjoyable

Studying God's Word should not be something to be

endured. Instead, a teacher should make learning a pleasure. As someone has said, "It's a sin to bore a kid with the Bible." And the results are devastating. God's Word is too important to treat as foul-tasting medicine or a painful innoculation.

If your junior highers enjoy studying the Bible in Sunday school, they will develop a love for God and His Word that will last a lifetime and will be translated into a life that pleases Him.

PRINCIPLE NO. 8
Teaching and learning are dependent upon the Holy Spirit

Without the Holy Spirit's working in both the teacher and the students, there will be no learning of Bible truths. He is the real teacher. Paul highlighted the importance of the Holy Spirit's teaching when he wrote the following words to the Corinthians: "Now we have received, not the spirit of the world, but the spirit which is of God; that we might know the things that are freely given to us of God. Which things also we speak, not in the words which man's wisdom teacheth, but which the Holy Ghost teacheth; comparing spiritual things with spiritual" (1 Corinthians 2:12,13).

The Holy Spirit is an integral part of teaching and learning:

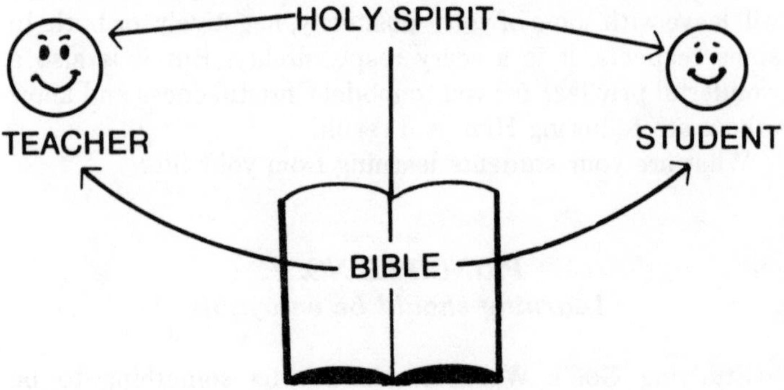

The Holy Spirit helps the teacher to do the following:

- understand the Bible passage he will teach and to practice it himself
- identify and relate students' needs to that passage
- choose methods which will involve students in understanding and applying the Biblical truths
- guide students in the learning process.

On the other side of the teaching/learning process, the Holy Spirit

- prepares students to be receptive to the truths they will study
- helps students to understand the Bible passage
- points out specific ways students can and should apply the Word
- strengthens students to practice the Biblical principles throughout the week.

QUICK REVIEW

1. Teaching is guiding students to discover for themselves.

T F

2. Learning is acquiring more facts.

T F

3. At the end of a class session, students should desire to obey God because the teacher said to.

T F

4. To promote growth, a teacher must help his students relate Biblical truths to their particular needs

and situations.

T F

5. If a student is interested, he is more likely to learn.

T F

6. Mental or physical involvement is necessary for learning to take place.

T F

7. When a student has learned a Biblical truth, he practices it and his life is changed.

T F

8. Bible study should be enjoyable.

T F

9. Teachers do not need the Holy Spirit's involvement in order to help students learn.

T F

Answers:

1. T 2. F 3. F 4. T 5. T 6. T 7. T 8. T 9. F

9 Lesson Preparation

The scouts do not have a corner on the motto, "Be prepared." It ought to be a byword for every Sunday school teacher too. Effective lesson preparation with the help of the Holy Spirit is one of the best guarantees of teaching which produces growth in the lives of students.

LESSON PLAN

Preparing a written lesson plan is similar to planning a vacation trip. When my husband and I take a vacation, we do not just get in the car and drive anywhere. Instead, we decide where we want to go, how to get there, how long it will take, where to stop along the way, and if we need to make motel reservations. A lesson plan will give you the same kind of specific direction, keep you from wasting time, guarantee that you will have all the supplies and equipment you need, and provide confidence.

Content

A written lesson plan should include the following items:

- Scripture—What are the main passages, related texts, and memory verse?
- Aim—What do you plan to accomplish?
- Presession—What will students who arrive early do?
- Approach—How will you capture your students' interests at the very beginning?

- Bible study—What does the passage say and what does it mean?
- Application—How can junior highers practice the truths studied and what one thing will each pupil do during the week?
- Timing—How long should each segment take?
- Materials needed—What supplies and equipment do you need?

The next section expands on these.

Procedure

Begin early in the week. Sunday afternoon or evening is not too soon to begin preparing for the following week; Wednesday is probably too late. It takes time to gather ideas, to be creative, to practice what you teach.

Schedule preparation time. Plan definite times to prepare; and allow sufficient time, about three to six hours. Leaving lesson preparation for odd moments when you have time usually means not getting to it until Saturday night.

Pray for God's wisdom and help as you prepare. Pray that your students will be present and receptive to the truth you study together. Pray for the class period that the study will be profitable and problems minimal.

Study. Before you read through the teacher's manual, study the Bible passage and related texts by answering the following questions:

- What does it say? (Observation step)
- What does it mean? (Interpretation step)
- What does it mean to me? to my students? (Application step)

The reference books listed in the Resources section in this chapter will help you to study and interpret. Reading the teacher's manual first shortchanges you out of firsthand discoveries of truth.

After your own study, read the manual and consult commentaries if necessary. Also read the student's book, and do the work required of your students.

Then proceed as follows:

Determine needs. Ask yourself, What needs of my students—either general needs of junior highers or specific needs of individuals—will this Bible passage or topic meet? Obviously every section of Scripture or topic will not meet all your students' needs, but there should be at least one point of intersection.

Write the aim. An aim is a statement of what you plan for your students to accomplish as a result of the Bible study. It grows out of both pupils' needs and Bible content, determines all the content to include, and guides in the selection of methods.

Read the aim in the teacher's manual located at the beginning of the lesson. Decide if it will meet your pupils' needs. If not, modify it or write a new one and base the rest of your lesson plan on it, choosing and deleting sections in the manual to accomplish it.

If you need to rework the aim, keep in mind the fact that a good aim has three qualities: 1) Brief enough to remember so you can keep it in mind while preparing and teaching; 2) clear enough to write down; 3) specific enough to achieve so you will know if you accomplish it or not. Be careful, however, of getting too specific; the aim needs to be flexible enough for the Holy Spirit to speak to individuals.

A good aim also has three parts which are closely related to one another: 1) Knowledge of Bible content; 2) desire to practice that knowledge; and 3) application of that truth, usually within a time limit of a week. Since the ultimate goal of teaching is changed lives, the emphasis should be on the doing.

The following is an example of an aim for junior highers from

Exodus 20:12, the fifth of the Ten Commandments:

I want my students to
KNOW—God commands us to honor and obey our parents
DESIRE—to honor and obey their parents
DO—honor and obey their parents in one way this week

Notice that each part has similar wording to make it easier to remember and that the DO section leaves room for the Spirit to direct each individual.

Develop the lesson. Using the teacher's manual as a guide, select content and methods for each segment of the lesson plan—approach, Bible study, and application. Estimate how much time each activity will take and adjust to fit your class period.

Begin with the Bible study section during which you will help students to discover what the passage says and what it means in order to accomplish the KNOW part of the aim. In Accent's curriculum, it is labeled "Communicating the Lesson." If you modified or changed the aim in the teacher's manual, you may need to refocus the study, deleting or adding to the suggestions in the manual. Also evaluate the methods suggested. Are they appropriate for your class? For example, if the manual recommends using small groups to study several Bible passages and you only have three students, you will need to use another method. Since learning is in proportion to doing, plan for as much student involvement as possible.

Next develop the application section. The teacher's manual gives suggestions for applying the principles and commands studied in the Bible passage(s). Again, if you changed the aim from the one in the manual, you may need to refocus the application. For the sample aim for Exodus 20:12 given above, you might ask the class for specific ways junior highers can honor and obey their parents, listing responses on the chalkboard or an overhead transparency.

Based on the possible applications, encourage students to choose one thing to do during the week in order to practice the Bible passage studied. This is the DO section of the aim. It is best to have junior highers write down what they will do so they do not forget. Sometimes there is a section for doing so in the Stretchsheet which is part of Accent's curriculum. Don't forget to check with your students during the week as well as the following Sunday to find out how they did—and to encourage them to follow through.

Finally, go back to the approach section. A teacher's manual usually includes a suggestion for getting your students' attention at the beginning of the class period. Determine if the suggestion in the manual will capture *your* students' attention. If not, plan an activity that will do so and lead naturally into the study. A transition sentence or a few statements should tie the approach into the Bible study.

If you need to change the approach activity, the following suggestions work well with junior highers: playing a song, discussing a picture or poster, asking a question, using a case study, responding to agree/disagree statements, listening to dialogues or monologues, playing charades, defining and describing a word on a graffiti sheet, using an object lesson, making a montage, or designing paper bumper stickers.

Plan presession. Instead of wasting the time before class officially begins, plan specific things to do with the students who arrive early. This is an opportunity to get better acquainted with pupils; to work on a class project, such as a banner; to review memory verses; to check on the assignment; etc.

Make a final copy of the lesson plan on half sheets of paper to fit into your Bible for convenience. Include time guidelines to keep you on track. Never take the teacher's manual to class; doing so gives the impression of not being prepared and of teaching a book instead of the Bible.

Gather materials. Make a list of all supplies and equipment needed at the top or end of the lesson plan. Then collect them and put everything in one place to take to class.

Evaluate. Go over the teaching session while it is fresh in your mind and evaluate it by one or more of the methods given under "Evaluation," later in this chapter.

RESOURCES

In addition to a teacher's manual, a publisher usually provides a packet of resources for preparing a lesson plan, but sometimes you may feel that it is wise to substitute some of your own aids to meet the special needs of your students. After all, even though the curriculum's resources are valuable, the writer did not know you and your class members and all their needs and abilities. Reference books and a teaching file can bridge the gap.

Reference Books

For personal Bible study of the text, especially a Bible book study for the quarter, a study guide focuses on details often missed. Irving Jensen's *Bible Self-Study Guides* (Moody Press) are excellent. The thirty-nine guides cover the whole Bible inductively, giving background information for each book. I have incorporated some of the charts and questions into my lesson plans. You can learn how to study the Bible inductively without a study guide through Jensen's *Enjoy Your Bible* (Moody Press). It teaches how to observe, interpret, and apply the Word, a process which will add personal insights to your lessons.

For information on Biblical people, objects, events, and concepts, consult a Bible dictionary or encyclopedia. My affordable favorites are *Unger's Bible Dictionary* by Merrill F. Unger (Moody Press); *Wycliffe Bible Encyclopedia* edited by Charles F. Pfeiffer, Howard F. Vos, and John Rea (2 vols., Moody Press); and *The Victor Handbook of Bible Knowledge* by V. Gilbert Beers (Victor Books). The information in the latter volume is arranged chronologically by Bible book. Sometimes I take these books to class and have students look up items pertaining to the lesson. The pictures help them to visualize unfamiliar things like Biblical instruments and architecture.

Part of the problem in understanding the Bible is the gap between that culture and ours. Books like *Manners and Customs of Bible Lands* by Fred H. Wight (Moody Press) and *Today's Handbook of Bible Times and Customs* by William L. Coleman (Bethany House) include explanations of such things as Jewish marriage and the agricultural methods of Bible times.

When geography is important to a lesson, consult an atlas which relates background information which helps students to imagine living there. *Baker's Bible Atlas* by Charles F. Pfeiffer (Baker Book House) and *The Wycliffe Historical Geography of Bible Lands* by Charles F. Pfeiffer and Howard F. Vos (Moody Press) are on my reference shelf.

Often studying related Bible passages adds extra insight to the lesson. *Strong's Exhaustive Concordance of the Bible* by James Strong (Abingdon Press) and *Nave's Topical Bible* by Orville J. Nave (revised and enlarged by S. Maxwell Coder, Moody Press) are useful. The concordance contains Greek and Hebrew dictionaries in the back to look up the original meanings of words.

For doctrinal studies, Emery H. Bancroft's *Elemental Theology* (revised by Ronald B. Mayers, Zondervan) outlines each of the major doctrines of the Bible. After studying his references, I can add more details to lessons.

For further help in interpretation of Bible texts, commentaries are valuable. Affordable, evangelical sets are *The Bible Knowledge Commentary* edited by John F. Walvoord and Roy B. Zuck (2 vols., Victor Books) and *Everyman's Bible Commentary Series* of paperbacks on specific Bible books (Moody Press).

For more ideas of methods to add variety to class time, check out *How to Do Bible Learning Activities*, grades 7-12, Book 1 by Ed Stewart and Neal McBride and Book 2 compiled by Rich Bundschuh and Annette Parrish (International Center for Learning). These handbooks explain over one hundred methods and are excellent for generating ideas.

Two other helpful handbooks of methods are Kenneth Gangel's *24 Ways to Improve Your Teaching* (Victor Books) and Marlene D. LeFever's *Creative Teaching Methods* (David C. Cook). *Visual Aid Encyclopedia*, compiled by Eleanor L. Doan (Regal Books) is a gold mine. More than 350 visuals are listed by subject (e.g., memory) and category (e.g., bulletin boards) with directions for making and using them.

Teaching File

My teaching file is the most helpful source of ideas to supplement my curriculum, especially when I modify or change the aim. It is a collection of materials and visuals on a wide variety of topics which are useful in teaching. A file, however, is only as good as the filing system. A terrific collection of materials is useless if you cannot readily find what you need. After several experiments with different filing systems, I have found the following one to be the most useful:

1) One or more drawers of topics in alphabetical order. The more specific the topic, the faster and easier it is to find what is needed. See the accompanying list of topic suggestions.

2) A section for Bible books in Biblical order. I have a folder for each book and for natural groups of books, such as Old Testament, Pentateuch, Prophets, New Testament, Gospels.

3) A section for pictures. These are primarily magazine, calendar and Sunday school paper pictures. See the accompanying list for suggestions.

4) A section for general visuals. This includes alphabet letters in envelopes according to size and style, tracing letters and stencils, maps, and patterns.

For the topical and Bible book sections, file anything and everything that would be useful in teaching a lesson on that subject or Bible passage. My file, for example, contains magazine articles, teaching visuals, illustrations, cartoons, applications, specific methods of teaching a subject, posters, sermon notes, tracts, booklets, overhead transparencies, and personal Bible study notes.

Topic Suggestions for a Teaching File

Bible characters—by name
Religions, cults, denominations—by name
Abortion
Adoption
Angels
Anger
Armor, Christian
Attitudes
Baptism
Beatitudes
Bible
Bible study
Body
Capital punishment
Christian liberty
Christian life
Christianity
Christmas
Church
Church attendance and actions
Citizenship
Communion
Communism
Conscience
Contentment
Covetousness
Creation/evolution
Criticism
Dancing
Dating
Death
Deceit
Decisions
Dedication
Depression
Disagreements
Disciples, twelve
Discipleship
Discipline
Divorce
Doubts
Dress
Drinking
Drugs
Easter
Eating disorders
Emotions
Encouragement
Envy
Eschatology
Evangelistic
Failure
Faith
Faithfulness
Family
Fantasy role games
Fear
Fellowship
Forgiveness
Freedom
Friendship
Fruit of the Spirit
Future
Gambling
Gifts of the Spirit
Giving
Goals
God the Father
God's will
Gossip
Guilt
Halloween
Heaven
Healing
Hell
Helping others
Holiness
Holy Spirit
Homosexuals
Honesty
Humanism
Humility

Insecurity
Jesus Christ—birth
Jesus Christ—life, ministry, character
Jesus Christ—death, resurrection, ascension
Joy
Judging
Judgment Seat of Christ
Laws
Leaders, leadership
Loneliness
Lordship of Christ
Lord's Prayer
Love
Love, romantic
Man
Marriage
Materialism
Meditation
Memorization
Mind
Miracles
Missions
Money
Movies
Music
Obedience
Occult
Parables
Parent-teen relationships
Patience
Peace
Peer pressure
Pharisees
Pornography
Praise
Prayer
Pride
Priorities
Problems
Quiet time
Repentance
Runaways
Salvation
Satan
Self-esteem
Selfishness
Separation
Service, servanthood
Sexual ethics
Shyness
Sin
Smoking
Speech
Stewardship
Stress
Success
Suffering
Suicide
Sunday
Swearing
Tabernacle
Teen pregnancy
Television
Temple
Temptation
Ten Commandments
Thankfulness
Thanksgiving
Time
Tongues, speaking in
Trials
Trinity
Values
Vocations
War
Wisdom
Witnessing
Women
Work
Worry
Worship

Topic Suggestions for a Picture File

Adults
Animals
Babies
Bible—Old Testament
Bible—New Testament
Buildings
Children
Christmas
Crowds
Easter, Palm Sunday
Evangelistic
Family
Graduation
Jesus Christ—birth and childhood
Jesus Christ—life and ministry
Jesus Christ—death, resurrection, ascension
Miscellaneous
Missions
Nature
Patriotic
School
Sports
Thanksgiving
Transportation
Weddings
Worship (churches, crosses, Bibles, prayer)
Youth

If you file the visuals and instruction sheets from the Accent teacher's resource packet, they will be easy to find to use with the same or other lessons. For instance, one packet includes among other things an overhead transparency on baptism, a large poster on courage, a copy master sheet on church membership, and an instruction sheet with an object lesson on salvation. These resources are excellent starters for a teaching file.

Some materials, such as large posters and visuals, do not fit in standard-size file folders. For these I include notes on the items in the appropriate folders so I do not forget I have them.

A four drawer, full suspension metal file cabinet is best for housing a file collection. Used files can be purchased for about half the price of new ones and spray-painted. Cardboard files and boxes also work but are not as sturdy or convenient. A blueprint file or cardboard under-the-bed storage boxes are useful for large visuals and posters.

The time it takes to set up a teaching file or to reorganize an existing one is more than gained back each week as you quickly locate additional help for preparing your lesson plans.

EVALUATION

Lesson planning does not end until after evaluation of the class period. Evaluation can be a frightening word or a welcome word, depending on how you view it. The Greek word means to test or examine for the purpose of approval and worthiness. In the New Testament, it almost always is used with the expectation of a positive result. Hence, evaluation should be a welcome word.

Purpose

Taking time to evaluate will help you to:

- discover your strengths for encouragement
- identify weak areas in which you need to improve
- determine if you achieved your aim or not
- ascertain how much your students are learning

Methods

There are many ways to evaluate teaching. The following five are some of the most helpful.

Each week while the class period is still fresh in your mind (such as Sunday afternoon), think through your teaching. Jot down on your lesson plan or a 3 x 5 card to attach to it: a one-word overall reaction (strong, good, fair, weak), two or three weaknesses and how you can correct them, two or three strengths, and student responses.

Another method is a more thorough self-evaluation, such as the "Self-Evaluation Test" on the next page.

A third way to evaluate is to invite someone to observe a class period and then discuss it with you afterwards. Choose a person who will be objective and is knowledgeable about teaching, such as your department superintendent or a trained teacher who is not teaching at the same time. Be sure to warn your class members ahead of time, telling them that person will be present to observe you, not them.

Giving your students a test is another means of evaluation. It may focus on Bible knowledge, attitudes, behavior, or all three areas. This method is especially good to use at the end of a course of study to determine what your students have learned.

Finally, you may want to ask your class members for their opinions. What did they like and dislike about a quarter's study? What suggestions do they have for improvement? If you have them write their answers anonymously, they will be more honest. Junior highers usually tell you more than you want to know, but their comments are helpful and often point out blind spots. You could reword most of the questions in the "Self-Evaluation Test" to prepare a form for your students to complete.

Follow-Up

After evaluating your lesson preparation and teaching, set goals for yourself. Focus on areas where you are weak, and list specific ways to turn those weaknesses into strengths. Then choose one area at a time and follow through. You can prepare now for the final exam at the Judgment Seat of Christ (1 Corinthians 3:10-15; 2 Corinthians 5:10)!

Self-Evaluation Test

1. Do I begin preparing for Sunday school class early in the week instead of cramming Saturday night?
2. Do I know the needs of my students and determine how the Bible passage or topic relates to them?
3. Do I have a specific, measurable aim each week? How well do I accomplish it?
4. Do the approaches capture my students' interests?
5. Do I actively involve my students in the Bible study instead of telling them what it says?
6. Do I guide my students to think of a variety of ways to apply Biblical truths in their lives?
7. Do I give my students meaningful assignments to encourage them to practice Biblical truth throughout the week? Do I check to find out how they did?
8. Do I use a variety of methods and audio-visual aids?
9. Do I use words and concepts which my junior highers can understand instead of talking over their heads or down to them?
10. What indications have my students given to show that they enjoy being in my class and studying the Bible?

Two areas in which I need to improve and specific steps I will take to do so:

Portions of this chapter originally appeared in *Moody Monthly* (November 1980) and *Success* (Summer 1981) and are reprinted here by permission.

QUICK REVIEW

1. A written lesson plan gives specific direction for the teaching time.

T F

2. It does not matter if I wait until the end of the week to prepare a lesson plan.

T F

3. Before reading the teacher's manual, it is best to study the Bible passage myself.

T F

4. Before planning the Bible study time, I need to decide how the passage relates to my students' needs and to write a specific aim.

T F

5. Every lesson plan should include an interesting approach and sufficient time for application.

T F

6. It does not matter if I take time to evaluate my teaching or not.

T F

Answers: 1. T 2. F 3. T 4. T 5. T 6. F

10 Teaching Methods

When I was going to college, I worked in a donut shop one summer. The pay was minimum wage and the hours were horrendous for a night person (4-11 a.m.), but there was one outstanding benefit. I could eat all the donuts I wanted for free. For someone who really liked donuts but rarely got them at home and who was desperate for a job, the offer sounded great. For two weeks I sampled donuts I had never seen before, put cream filling in unfilled peanut butter sticks, pigged out on my favorite kinds, and gained weight. The third week I couldn't stand the thought of eating another donut. Too much of a good thing was just too much.

The same is true in teaching. Young teens get bored with the same methods week after week, especially if those methods do not involve them in the learning process. Curriculum materials are designed to provide that variety in teaching and challenge students to interact with and apply the Bible passages you study together. The following explanations will help you to use those materials more effectively and to choose different methods if necessary.

QUESTION AND ANSWER

Questions of various kinds by themselves and linked with other methods form the backbone of student learning. They encourage students to study the Scripture passage for themselves and to apply its teaching to their daily lives.

With questions and answers, the teacher asks the question and the students respond back to the teacher as illustrated in this diagram (T = teacher, S = student):

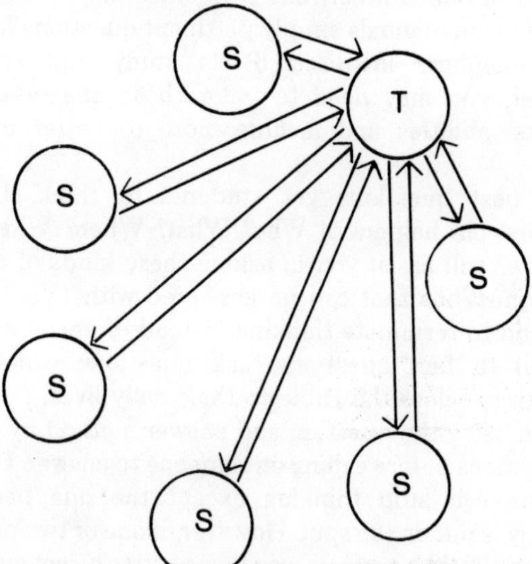

In discussion, students respond to one another as well as to the teacher, like this:

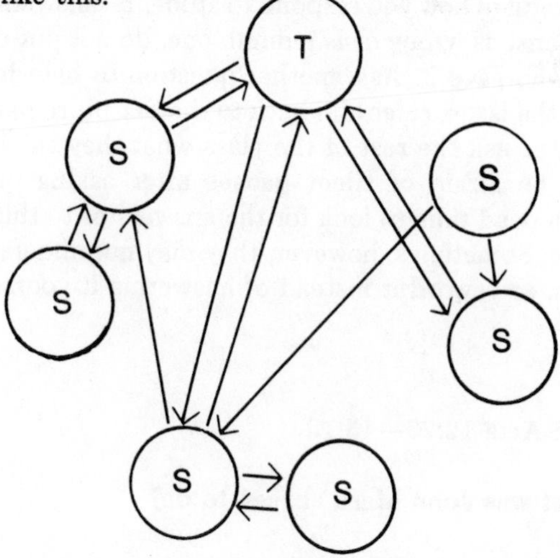

Young teens can answer fact and thought questions well; but generally they are not good discussers, especially seventh graders. Younger junior highers rarely react to the remarks and opinions of one another, but older ones may.

Curriculum manuals supply pertinent questions for guiding group members in direct Bible study and application. However, you may need to tailor those questions to your students' abilities and include more to better meet their needs.

The best questions get students to think. Using the reporters' old helpers of Who? What? When? Where? Why? and How? will assist you in asking these kinds of questions. Avoid questions that can be answered with "Yes" or "No"; they tend to terminate thinking instead of encouraging it. In addition to fact questions, ask questions which require students to relate the Bible to their daily lives.

When using the question and answer method by itself, ask the questions before calling on someone to answer. Otherwise, everyone can stop thinking except the one person who suddenly is put on the spot. However, if one or two pupils tend to monopolize the answers, you may need to direct questions to specific individuals for a while.

Be careful of how you respond to students' answers. Even if the response is wrong or is a dumb one, do not put down the person who gave it. Ask another question to help him think through the issue, refer him back to the Scripture passage for support, or ask the rest of the class what they think.

Don't be afraid of silent pauses after asking questions. Students need time to look for the answers or to think about the topic. Sometimes, however, they may not understand the question, so reword it instead of answering it yourself.

Samples

Passage: Acts 12:25—13:13

- What was John Mark chosen to do?

- What do you think his responsibilities were on this trip?
- What did Paul, Barnabas, and John Mark do on this trip?
- What happened at Paphos?
- Shortly after that, what did John Mark do?
- Why do you think he gave up and went home?

Passage: Acts 15:36-39

- Why did Paul and Barnabas want to take another missionary trip?
- Who did Barnabas want to take with them?
- How did Paul feel about Barnabas' choice?
- Why do you think Paul objected so much?
- Why do you think Barnabas wanted to take John Mark when he had quit the last time?
- What might have happened to John Mark if Barnabas hadn't had faith in him?
- What do you learn from Barnabas' choice and actions?

Passage: Exodus 20:15; Ephesians 4:28

- What would your definition of stealing be?
- In the light of 1 Corinthians 16:2 what kind of theft do God's people sometimes commit?
- What types of stealing do you think are the biggest temptations to the young person today?
- How do you think it is possible for a Christian young person to avoid the kinds of stealing just mentioned?
- What advice would you give a school friend who came to you and confessed he had been shoplifting, but now was a Christian who wanted to make things right but was afraid a confession would ruin his testimony?

Passage: Exodus 20:8-11; Mark 2:23—3:10

- Your parents disagree with you on the type of music you listen to. What is your attitude regarding their feelings?
- Your parents don't like your friends. What reasons would you give for this?
- Have you ever said, "My parents just don't understand me. They are so old-fashioned!" Why do you feel this way?
- Your parents don't attend church; in fact, they have never accepted Jesus Christ as their personal Savior. How would you handle this situation?

BUZZ GROUPS

Buzz groups are several small groups of three to six students who meet to answer assigned questions or to research a topic. After the members of each group have completed their study, they report their findings to the rest of the class. This method involves more students than when questions are directed to the whole class since it is more difficult to observe instead of participating when in a smaller group.

The group dynamics of this method look like this:

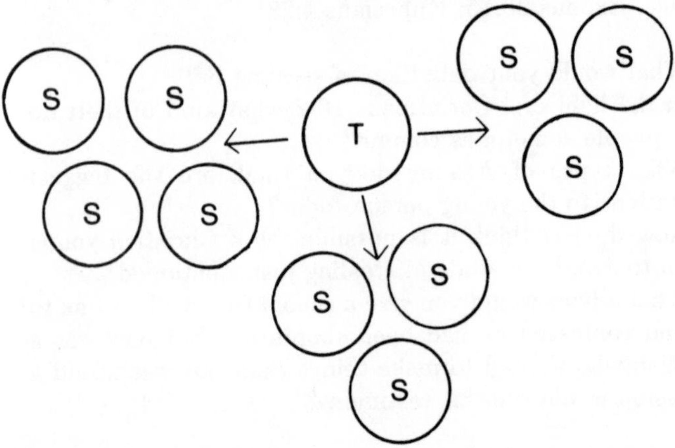

The use of buzz groups involves the following steps:

1) Write out the assignments for each group. These may be indicated in the teacher's manual. In Accent's curriculum, assignments appear in the Stretchsheets, ready for distribution as directed by the teacher's manual.

2) Divide the class into groups, appoint leaders, and distribute the assignments along with the tools needed (i.e., pencils, reference books).

3) Set a time limit for the groups to meet, allowing enough time to complete the study. Setting a kitchen timer helps the groups to be conscious of the amount of time left. Give a three to five minute warning before time is up.

4) While the groups meet, circulate to answer questions, check on their progress, and keep them on track.

5) When the time is up, call for reports from each group and fill in any details they missed.

Sample

Topic: Timothy

Group 1: Read 2 Timothy 1:5; 3:15 and Acts 16:1. What was Timothy's homelife like? How was it the same as or different from yours?

Group 2: Read 1 Timothy 4:12; 5:23; 2 Timothy 1:7-8 and Acts 16:2. What kind of a person was Timothy? (What was he like?) In what ways was he like you?

(If you have four groups, give each assignment to two groups.)

INDUCTIVE SCRIPTURE SEARCH

Inductive Scripture search is both the foundation and the combination of methods which involve questions. It requires students to study the Bible passage(s) directly in order to make their own findings instead of being spoon-fed by the teacher.

There are three basic steps to inductive study:

- Observation—What does the passage say? During this step students gather the facts.
- Interpretation—What does the passage mean? Using reference books, pupils seek to understand those facts.
- Application—What does the passage mean to me? Students decide how they can apply the principles and commands to their lives today.

Just these three questions can be used to lead class members to study a section of Scripture. See "Sample of Inductive Scripture Search for Mark 16:1-8." Most junior highers, however, need more specific questions to help them. Good curriculum materials generally include questions and activities for all three steps even though they are not labeled as such. Search them out and use them in this way.

When time is limited and you want to study a number of Bible references, write each reference on a slip of paper and distribute the papers to individuals or pairs. Have them read the verses and answer the question(s).

NEIGHBOR NUDGING

Neighbor nudging is a mini-version of buzz groups. For this method, students turn to the person next to them and answer an assigned question for a few minutes. After the time is up, each pair shares their responses with the whole group; or if the group is large, several volunteers tell their answers.

Neighbor nudging can be used to approach a lesson topic, to study a portion of Scripture, or to discover possible ways to apply Biblical truth. This method is a good alternative to use when there is not enough time for buzz groups. It provides maximum participation since every student must respond to the question.

Samples

- What qualities make a good friend? In other words, what is a good friend like? (Approach question.)
- Read Colossians 1:9-12. What were Paul's prayer requests for the Colossian believers? (Bible study question.)
- How can you demonstrate love this week? (Application question.)

The group for neighbor nudging will look like the following illustration:

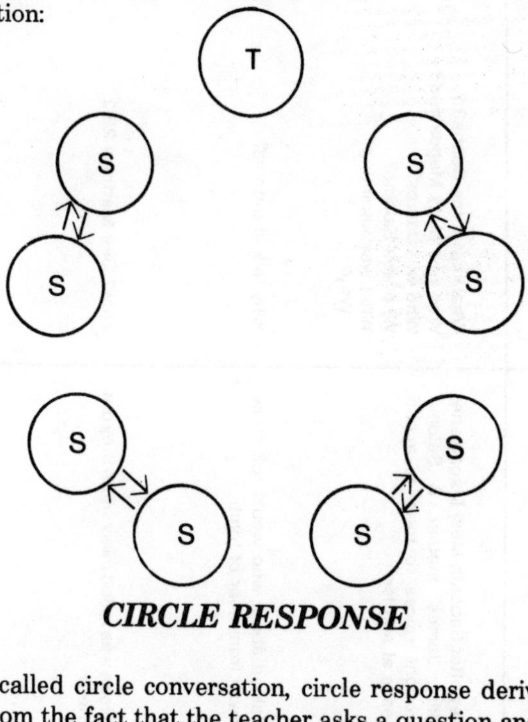

CIRCLE RESPONSE

Also called circle conversation, circle response derives its name from the fact that the teacher asks a question and goes around the circle or group to get a response from everyone.

Sample of Inductive Scripture Search for Mark 16:1-8

OBSERVATION What does it say?	INTERPRETATION What does it mean?	APPLICATION What does it mean to me?
Day after Sabbath Mary Magdalene; Mary, James' mother, & Salome brought spices to tomb to anoint Jesus at sunrise	What day is the Sabbath? Who was Mary Magdalene? Who was James? Who was Salome? What was anointing? Why?	
Talked about who would roll stone away from door of tomb	Why talk about this?	
Stone was rolled away when they got there	How? See Matthew 28:2.	Lord sometimes takes care of problems before we get to the situation; we worry for nothing

They went into tomb & were amazed to see a young man in long white garment sitting on right side	Who was this man? See Matthew 28:2-3. Who are amazed? What were they expecting?	Evidences for bodily Resurrection: 1) stone rolled away 2) not in tomb 3) message of angel to women
Man knew they were looking for Jesus who was crucified & said He was risen & not there	What does this verse teach about Jesus?	
Man told them to go tell the disciples & Peter that they could see Jesus in Galilee as he said to them	Why single out Peter? Where is Galilee? When did he tell them this? See Mark 14:28.	
Women left quickly & fled because they trembled & were amazed; didn't tell anyone because they were afraid	Why were they afraid?	My response to the Resurrection is:

This method is best used with opinion questions to which there are no right or wrong answers. That way no one is embarrassed by his response and everyone can contribute. It is a good way to begin the lesson time to get everyone involved and thinking right away. For example, "What is one of your biggest temptations?" Circle response also can be used to conclude the Bible study to obtain a number of ways to apply the truths with a question like "What is one way young teens can serve the Lord?" The student book sometimes includes questions which are appropriate for this method.

The method looks like this:

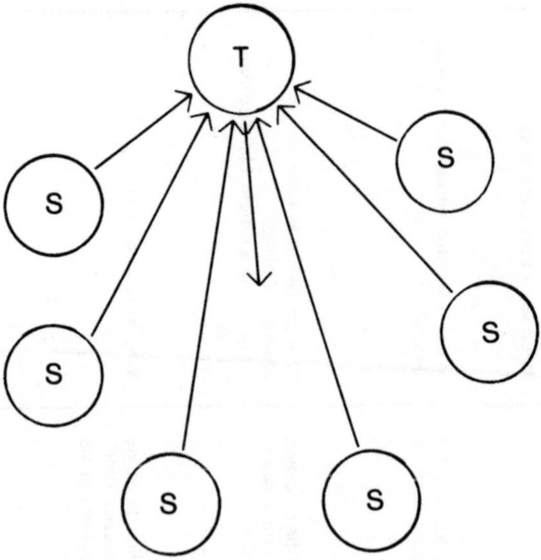

Samples:

- Name one person or thing we can praise God for.
- What is one way junior highers can serve the Lord?
- How can we help someone this week?
- What is one of your biggest problems in living

the Christian life?

INTERVIEW

During an interview, one person or a group asks questions of another person(s) in order to acquire information or ideas.

Interviews primarily are associated with asking questions of live people, either in person or on tape. For example, the teacher's manual may suggest that you invite a deacon to class and have students interview him to find out what the deacons do.

When planning to interview someone, have pupils write out questions ahead of time, instructing them to avoid questions which can be answered with "Yes" or "No." This step will prevent embarrassing silence when the group faces the person.

Interviewing is not limited to people who are living, however. You can adapt the curriculum materials to ask questions of Bible characters and then answer them. To do so, have one or more students take the role of the Biblical person and the rest of the class become the interviewers. With young teens, it usually is better to divide the class evenly between the two roles. Instruct the people being interviewed to study the Bible passage in order to answer questions. At the same time have the interviewers study the passage and write questions to ask, thinking in terms of Who? What? When? Where? Why? and How?.

During the interview, those who are taking the part of the Biblical person should speak in the first person and the interviewers should address them as if they really were that person. Let those being interviewed use their Bibles if needed to answer questions. The group dynamics of this type of interviewing look like the following diagram:

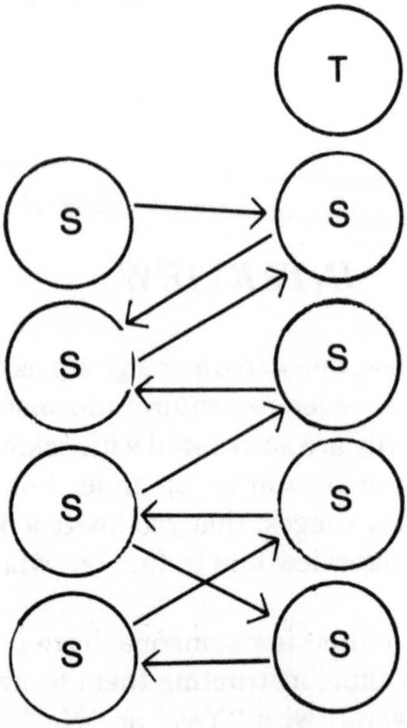

If you have a student who is capable of answering questions alone, you may want to set up the situation like a television or radio talk show with questions from the audience (class).

After God called Gideon to deliver Israel from the Midianites, he gathered an army for the fight. In order to find out what happened, divide the class into three groups and assign each group one of these passages from Judges: 7:1-25; 8:1-17; 8:22-35. Then divide each of the three groups into Gideon(s) and interviewers. Questions and answers could include the following:

7:1-25

- Why did God say you had too many men? (He was afraid we would become boastful and take the credit for the victory instead of giving it to Him.)
- How did you reduce the number of soldiers? (I sent home

everyone who was afraid. Then I tested the rest by bringing them to the water. I sent home all the men who kneeled down to drink and kept the 300 who lapped the water by putting their hands to their mouths.)

• How did you feel about fighting the Midianites? Why? (I was afraid because they were stronger and in control.)

• How did you overcome this fear? (I went down to their camp with my servant and heard a dream one of the Midianites had and its interpretation that I would conquer them. Then I knew I didn't need to be afraid.)

• What weapons did you use to fight the Midianites? (Trumpets, pitchers, and torches.)

• What was your battle strategy? (We surrounded the Midianite camp; blew our trumpets; broke our pitchers with the torches inside; and cried, "The sword of the Lord, and of Gideon.")

• What happened? (They ran.)

• What tribes helped you to capture and kill the Midianites? (Naphtali, Asher, and Manasseh.)

8:1-17

• Why were the Ephraimites upset with you? (Because I didn't ask them to help me fight the Midianites.)

• How did you answer them? (I told them that their capturing of the Midianite leaders, Oreb and Zeeb, was just as important.)

• Why didn't the men of Succoth and Penuel give you bread when you asked for it? (They were afraid of the kings of Midian in case I didn't capture them.)

• How did you punish them later? (I disciplined the elders of Succoth with thorns and tore down the tower of Penuel and killed all the men there.)

8:22-35

• To whom did the people of Israel give the credit for

victory? (Me.)

• What did the Israelites want you to do? (Rule over them.)

• What was your response? (I told them, "No, the Lord will rule over you.")

• What did you do instead? What happened? (I made an ephod out of gold earrings and put it in Ophrah. The people "played the harlot" with it.)

• How long was Israel free? (Forty years.)

ROLE PLAYING

To role play, two or more students act out a situation or relationship with no script or preparation. They put themselves into another person's shoes in order to understand his position, point of view, or feelings. The following diagram illustrates the group dynamics of this method:

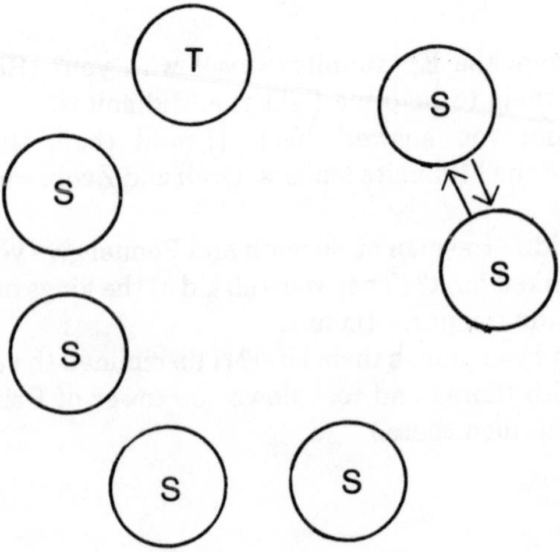

To use role playing, follow these steps:

1) Ask for volunteers to play the various roles.

2) Give each participant brief written instructions from the teacher's manual to identify the situation and his character. Allow a couple of minutes for the volunteers to think themselves into those roles.

3) Introduce the situation to the class.

4) The participants then start speaking, making up the dialogue and actions as they go and reacting to each other's comments.

5) After a few minutes, cut off the conversation. Ask the participants how they felt in that situation. Have the group evaluate the dialogue and actions by asking such questions as, "Why did the conversation go the way it did?" "How could the reactions have been changed?"

Role play is a good approach method to interest students in studying the Bible topic or passage. After the end of the Bible study, you can redo the role play situation as it ought to be, incorporating the Biblical truths studied.

Students can role play Bible characters, too, to explore how they might have felt in various situations. Instead of making up dialogue, they talk about the person's feelings, problems, and thoughts which he or she might have had.

Samples:

- Modern situation

Directions for Sue: You can't find your new sweater that you saved your allowance and babysitting money for two months to buy. You've just finished searching your room for the second time. Frustrated, you decide to check the family room again. As you pass the living room, your sister Cathy enters the house wearing your sweater. There's a dirt stain on the sleeve. You are frustrated and light into her.

Directions for Cathy: You had to have a green sweater for a skit at school today. Since you don't own one, you wanted to ask Sue this morning if you could borrow her new one. She had already left for school so you took it, thinking she would understand since she lent you clothes before. When you come home from school, Sue will see you in her sweater and be mad at you.

Directions for the class: Sue has been looking for her new sweater when her sister comes home wearing it.

- Biblical situation

After reading Luke 1:26-35 and discussing the situation, say to the group: Put yourself in Mary's shoes for a few minutes. How do you think she felt when the angel told her she was going to give birth to God's Son when she wasn't even married? What are some of the problems she faced? What questions might have gone through her mind?

QUICK REVIEW

1. Questions should get students to look at the Bible text and to think about the implications of the text.
T F

2. It is best to call on an individual before asking the questions so he or she can be ready.
T F

3. If someone answers incorrectly, help him to find the right answer in the text or ask the rest of the class to answer too.
T F

4. If no one answers a question right away, you should tell the class the answer.
T F

5. Buzz groups encourage more students to participate in answering questions than directing questions

to the whole group.

T F

6. The best questions for circle response are opinion questions with no right or wrong answers.

T F

7. Role plays have written scripts for all the participants.

T F

8. Inductive Scripture search starts with beliefs and seeks to prove them from the Bible.

T F

9. Scripture search replaces spoon-feeding by a teacher.

T F

Answers:

1. T 2. F 3. T 4. F 5. T 6. T 7. F 8. F 9. T

11 *Aids to Better Teaching*

Part of surviving as a teacher of junior highers is planning variety and student involvement for class time. To help you do so, incorporate some of the following teaching aids in your class sessions or as extra activities.

AUDIO-VISUALS

Young teens have grown up on television, films, and radio. They are bombarded on all sides with audio-visual media. Students generally remember fifty percent of what they see and hear combined. That fact alone should motivate teachers to visualize and to incorporate sounds other than their voices as much as possible. Here are some ideas:

- Pictures

  Pictures can help students to bridge the cultural gap between them and Biblical times, to explore feelings and reactions in everyday situations.

- Cartoons

  Comic strips, especially Peanuts, sometimes focus on Biblical themes.

- Chalkboard

  List students' responses to questions, write out assignments, draw diagrams.

- Flannelboard

Cut strips and shapes from paper towels and write on them with marking pens. They adhere to the board without any special backing.

- Maps

Buy commercial maps or sketch your own on poster board to enlarge the area on which you are focusing. If you cover a map with clear Con-Tact paper, you can write on it with water-soluble markers and wash it off.

- Flip chart

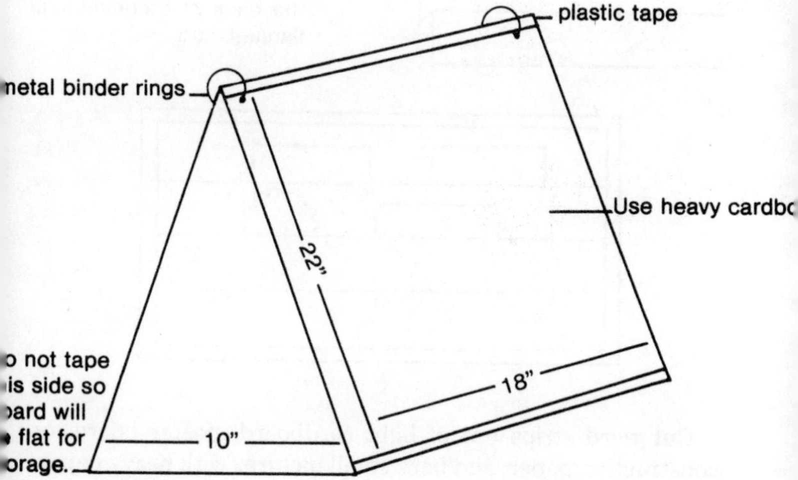

You can buy drawing pads with blank paper large enough for this chart. Or use newspaper want ads without a lot of pictures on which to write words or phrases.

- Montage

Cut pictures and words from magazines to illustrate a topic. Arrange, and rubber cement them on a length of shelf paper. Let the students make a montage for an approach or application activity.

- Pocket chart

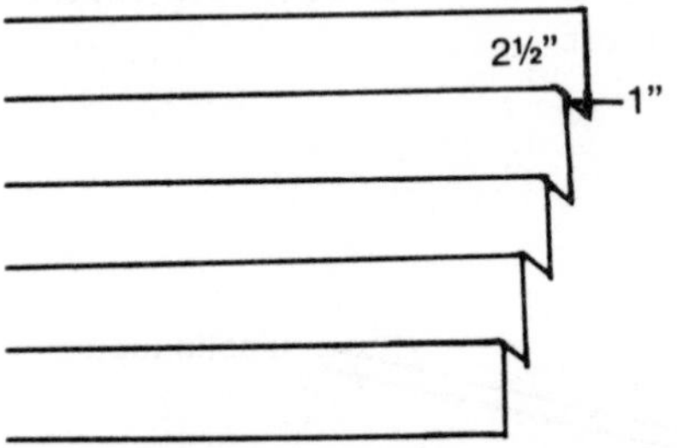

Fold heavy brown paper or Con-Tact paper with squares (leave the backing on) as shown. Tape all the edges to a 24" x 36" piece of heavy cardboard with plastic tape. Or make it to fit the back of a commercial flannelboard.

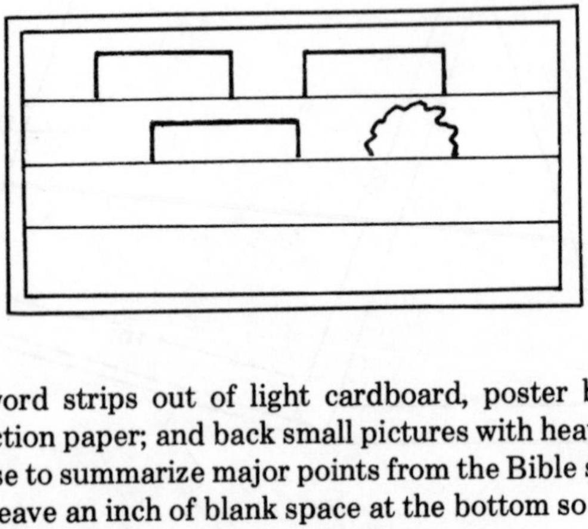

Cut word strips out of light cardboard, poster board, or construction paper; and back small pictures with heavy paper. Use these to summarize major points from the Bible study. Be sure to leave an inch of blank space at the bottom so words or pictures are not covered by the pocket.

- Posters

Buy commercial ones, or make your own with magazine pictures and poster board.

- Charts and graphs

Chart a Bible character's spiritual life to show his or her ups and downs in order to help students better identify with that person.

- Overhead Projector

This versatile teaching aid has an advantage over many others, as it projects on a screen pictures, cartoons, maps, diagrams, and allows for writing on the transparencies as a lesson or discussion progresses. Most Christian bookstores carry printed transparencies on many Bible subjects, as well as maps and teaching posters. Accent Publications includes colorful transparencies related to the lessons in each Junior High Teacher's Classroom Kit.

- Filmstrip, film, video cassette
- Slides

Show appropriate 35 mm slides, or make your own with write-on slides. (See below.)

PROJECTS

These types of learning projects add the element of doing to seeing and hearing, thus greatly increasing retention of Biblical truth.

Bible Newspaper

Historical or narrative Bible books or portions (i.e., Gospels, Acts, Genesis, Numbers, Old Testament historical books, sections of Old Testament prophets) can be summarized or reviewed in the form of a newspaper or any part of it. For example, one of my classes reviewed a quarter's study of the book of Judges through news stories, interviews, editorials, picture "photographs," advertisements, want ads, and a crossword puzzle. Together we chose the name *Judges Journal.* I laid out the stories and art to look like a newspaper with headlines and bylines and then duplicated copies for the whole church.

The same method can be used on a smaller scale for only one lesson. Or instead of producing a newspaper, write and tape a newscast, adding lines for an anchor to tie it all together.

Banner

Students can illustrate their discoveries from the Bible text with felt figures and letters glued onto burlap to make one or more banners. Have each individual or buzz group cut appropriate shapes or free forms from felt squares, write on them with marking pens, and glue them to hemmed burlap pieces with white craft glue.

Song Writing

A class can compose original songs by writing new words to a familiar hymn tune to teach the content and/or application of a Bible passage or topic. After studying the passage, divide the class into smaller groups and have each group write a stanza, substituting one syllable for each note and softly singing it out loud to be sure it is singable. Or a small class can work together to write a song. When finished, decide on a title, write a chorus if needed, and sing it together. Duplicate copies for everyone.

The following song was written by a class of junior highers from their study of 1 Kings 17:1-7.

Elijah at the Brook

Tune: "Amazing Grace"

1. Elijah brought a message to
The wicked King Ahab.
"There won't be rain or dew these years;
This is what God has said."

2. God sent Elijah to the brook
To hide from King Ahab.
God sent the ravens to feed him
So that he would not die.

3. He learned that God could keep him safe,
And how to trust in Him.
He also learned that God loved him
And how to be patient.

Write-On Slide Presentation

Using blank write-on slides (Kodak markets them in boxes of 100, available at camera or audio-visual stores) and water soluble overhead transparency markers, your class can put together a presentation to share what they are learning with the rest of the church. Have students draw simple pictures (stick figures are fine) and write words with fancy borders on the slide surface.

You or your students can write a script, or you may want to choose a recorded song.

When slides are finished, put them in a slide tray, mark the script for advances, and practice showing it with students reading the script. Arrange to show your presentation in a church service.

Actual size

Write-on slides also can be used for one or two sessions and shown immediately instead of as a review project. For example, introduce the topic by having each student make a few slides; then show them with appropriate Scripture verses or recorded song.

REVIEW GAMES

Quarterly reviews become interesting and exciting when they are in the form of a game. Possibilities include the following:

- Original board games

When adapting games, substitute questions or words from the Bible passages you have studied. With original games, limit the number of questions to about twenty in order to review the content several times during the class period. You may want to require pupils to answer questions correctly before moving and to read the Bible references included with the questions out loud if they do not know the answers. For all games, include both fact and application questions.

- Adaptation of television game shows, such as Jeopardy, Password, What's My Line?

Sample:

Daniel Jeopardy

Instructions: Divide the class into three teams. Choose a starting team by drawing numbers. One person from the starting team chooses a category and amount. Remove the point card to reveal the statement underneath. The first person to stand gets to answer the question; the answer must be in the form of a question and pertain to the category. If that person answers incorrectly, his team loses the points and the person from the next team who stands gets to answer. One person cannot answer more than two questions in a row; he must sit out a question.

The person who answers the question correctly chooses the next category and amount. Allow eight to ten minutes for each half of the game and one minute for the final answer. For the final category, each team chooses one member to answer. He writes his answer on a card. The team with the most points wins.

The game board can be put on poster board, chalkboard, or overhead transparencies and covered with cards which indicate the points for each question. In the first half of the game the questions in each category are worth 10, 20, 30, 40, 50 points in descending order; in the second half they are worth double; the final question is 200 points.

Sample game board:

DANIEL & FRIENDS	THE GOLD IMAGE	SCHOOL DAYS	THE LION'S DEN
Hananiah, Mishael, Azariah	Cast into a fiery furnace	Purposed that he wouldn't defile himself	Third ruler of Babylon during Daniel's life
Belteshazzar	Shadrach, Meshach & Abed-nego	Pulse and water	Faithful, no faults or errors
Their nationality	God	Three years	Be cast into lion's den
As captives	Three men bound and four men loose	Learning and tongue of Chaldeans	Decree made to remove Daniel
One reason they were honored	Signal to bow down to idol	No blemish, well-favored, wise, knowledgeable, understand science	Darius' reaction to accusation against Daniel

Final category: Dream Interpretation
Question: Principle upon which Daniel interpreted the king's dream

• Adaptation of commercial games

Sample: Fruit of the Spirit Tic-Tac-Toe

Instructions: Divide the class into two teams, and choose one to begin. The first person on that team picks a category. If he answers the question pertaining to that subject correctly, his team puts an X or an 0 in that square. Then the first person on the next team takes his turn. The first team to get three X's or 0's in a row wins.

Prepare several questions for each category.

Sample board:

Patience	Gentle-ness	Fruit
Faithful-ness	Hodge-Podge	Meekness
Holy Spirit	Temper-ance	Goodness

QUICK REVIEW

1. Using audio-visuals is important to help pupils to understand and retain Biblical truth.

T F

2. Only teachers of young children should use teaching aids like a chalkboard, pictures, and maps.

T F

3. Projects like making a newspaper involve students in doing something creative with the truth they study, thus promoting greater retention of it.

T F

4. Playing games in Sunday school is a waste of time.

T F

5. An interested student is learning something.

T F

Answers:

1. T 2. F 3. T 4. F 5. T

12 *Inside and Outside the Classroom*

Time for a quicky quiz. (But nobody will grade you!) The question is: What do teachers do in relation to their classes besides prepare lesson plans to teach once a week?

How did you do? Could you name at least six things? Teaching involves much more than one hour on Sunday morning, as you already have discovered if you are teaching. This chapter focuses on some of those other aspects of a teaching ministry.

GETTING ACQUAINTED WITH STUDENTS

There is no substitute for knowing each student personally. To be an effective teacher requires knowledge of individual needs, abilities, and interests as well as building relationships with students. The following steps will help you to get to know those junior highers who constitute your class.

Interviews

Soon after promotion, or whenever new students join your class, interview each one. So no one will feel threatened, announce that you will meet for five or ten minutes with each new student, asking everyone the same questions. The best times to talk are before and after class. Instead of scheduling appointments, talk with one or two who arrive early and ask a volunteer to stay after class.

When interviewing, find out about the pupil's family, school life, and spiritual life. You also may want to ask for suggestions for class time. See the "Personal Interview Questions" form for specific questions.

I have found that I learn more than answers to my questions. Students usually disclose attitudes and information about other areas of their lives. Often a pupil who does not participate in class converses freely when there are just the two of us. Mary, for example, rarely spoke in class. But during the interview she talked almost nonstop for fifteen minutes. Pam revealed many insecurities while detailing her life history.

Home Visits

The next step in getting acquainted is home visits. In order to prepare parents and save fruitless trips, phone for an appointment at least a week in advance, making certain both

Personal Interview Questions

What is your birthdate?

What are your parents' first names (and last name if different) and occupations? Do you live with both parents? If not, what is the situation?

What are your brothers' and sisters' names and ages? Which ones live with you?

What school do you attend? What time do you get home from school?

What activities, such as sports and clubs are you involved in at school and elsewhere?

What subjects do you like best? Least?

parents and student will be home.

During the visit, ask the parents about their work and interests, seeking to get acquainted. Explain what you do in class and how their child responds. On subsequent visits to a home, discuss their junior higher's spiritual growth—or lack of it—if the parents are Christians. This is also a good time to detect the effectiveness of your teaching methods from both pupils and parents.

Although you should focus on reporting positive qualities, sometimes it becomes necessary to discuss a problem. When Jane, for instance, entered my class, she did not participate. Her mother explained that Jane did not talk to people until she knew them well. She was afraid to fail and so did nothing. As a result, I looked for every opportunity to praise Jane and try to involve her in non-threatening situations. After about a year

---

Tell me about your salvation experience—when, where, circumstances. When and where were you baptized? When did you become a church member?

Describe your present relationship with the Lord.

How often do you read the Bible? Pray? Read the student manual and answer the questions? Learn the weekly memory verse?

Are you involved in the church's club program and/or youth group?

What personal prayer requests do you have?

What suggestions do you have for our class?

---

she became one of the best participators in class discussion.

Also ask the parents for any information which will help in teaching their children. After Carla's mother explained her daughter's reading problem, I knew not to embarrass her by asking her to read aloud or explain a verse after silent reading.

Frequently you will discover the causes of problems by observing the home atmosphere and parent-child interaction. The yelling and confusion at Pam's house explained her bad disposition on some Sunday mornings.

"Let's Get Acquainted" Form

While talking to parents at home, ask students to fill out a "Let's Get Acquainted" sheet. Or have them do so at another time. It focuses on such areas as abilities, hobbies, relationship with parents, and Christian living. For specific questions, see the form, "Let's Get Acquainted." From the answers you will be able to match students' interests and abilities with class projects. When you need posters, you know who would like to make them. When role playing is part of the lesson, you know who is interested in acting.

The answers to the questions on Christian living reveal weak areas which you can emphasize and offer Biblical help for in appropriate lessons. For example, when Lynn completed this sheet, she admitted her temper bothers her most. Several girls wrote that they felt God was displeased with their lack of Bible study, prayer, and obedience. I was able to incorporate those needs into the application of a lesson on God's working in our lives.

To make the form on the next page, type the questions on an 8½ x 11-inch sheet of paper with space to answer each one.

Class Socials

Another way to get acquainted is through quarterly class socials. Junior highers enjoy bowling, miniature golf, picnics, bike hikes, ball games, playing games, and all-nighters. Asking

Let's Get Acquainted

Name:

Place a check after the things you like to do: art work ______, writing ______, making posters ______, acting ______.

What instrument(s) do you play?

What are your hobbies, collections, special interests, and abilities?

What career are you interested in?

Briefly describe your parents and your relationship with them.

What one thing bothers you the most in your Christian life?

Do you think the way you dress and act at school glorifies the Lord? Why or why not?

Are you afraid to witness? Why or why not?

What three things do you think God is most pleased with in your life?

What three things do you think God is displeased with in your life?

What bugs you the most?

your class members to each list five activities they would like to do will yield more ideas than you will have time for.

Even a simple dinner at your house and table games or a barbecue at a park offers rich insights. As you talk and play together, observe the students interacting with one another. Lynn, for instance, was a leader in class but usually was ignored at socials. During such times she shared her hurt with me. As a result, I was able to personalize lessons to deal with this problem.

Taking students to dinner in groups of two or three is a productive get-acquainted activity. Fast-food and pizza restaurants are easy on the budget and preferred by junior highers. Pupils share their problems more freely in a smaller group and feel more at ease with a friend or two along. They also have an opportunity to ask you questions about yourself.

As I have talked with students in this setting, I have been able to detect spiritual progress or problems. Dianna told me about her struggle in living for the Lord at school and asked for specific help and prayer. Bonnie's lack of interest in spiritual things was apparent from her conversation but had not been noticeable in class.

Records

Keep a notebook with pages for each student to record all the answers from the interviews and get-acquainted forms as well as observations noted throughout the year. The notebook then becomes a prayer book and a source of information in order to personalize lessons.

CLASSROOM MANAGEMENT

Although junior highers do not present as many discipline problems as young children, you can expect some, such as talking, fooling around with purses and other items, and mild "goof-off" behavior. Most of these problems should be ignored; they are part of being a junior higher. Sometimes the behavior does get out of hand, however; but there are several keys to eliminating most behavior problems.

An obvious—but sometimes overlooked—key is specific prayer for the students, the classroom situation, and wisdom to cope. God is still greater than any discipline problems you may encounter and wants to help with the situations.

Another important key is involving students in the Bible study. Junior highers who are expected to sit quietly through a long lecture will manufacture their own entertainment and consequent disruptions. But students who are involved are usually too busy and interested to disrupt.

Sometimes the classroom itself causes problems. Too much heat or lack of it, overcrowded conditions, drab or overly bright colored walls, and disorderliness all contribute to behavior problems. Study your classroom, and take steps to eliminate any of these conditions which are present.

Teachers who build a personal relationship with each teen also cut down on the need to discipline. Junior highers who know and respect their teacher are less likely to goof off in class.

I have found it very helpful to establish a few—with emphasis on few—rules at the beginning of each Sunday school year. One rule is that students do not share or play around with items not being used in the study activities, such as combs or pictures. Violators lose the item until the following week. For the first month, I issue warnings so everyone is aware of the rule. I have had to collect only a few items and never twice from the same student. The other rule we have in class is no excessive taking about subjects other than the topic of study. There will always be some talking, but I ignore the short remarks. Occasionally I need to tell a student to save the conversation for after class. It is important to remember that rules are useless if they are not enforced.

If excessive talking or goofing around persists and cannot be ignored, it is best to have a talk with the offenders. Do this privately so you do not embarrass them in front of the group and lose their respect. Let them know you like having them in class but their behavior is disrupting to studying God's Word. Ask for their cooperation, making it clear—with a loving attitude—that you will not tolerate the misbehavior. I have used this tactic a few times; and in each instance, the request for cooperation solved the problem.

A student who is extremely disruptive usually is seeking attention. If so, give him extra affirmation and responsibilities without making him and the rest of the group feel that he is the teacher's pet. Often a visit to the home yields clues to class misbehavior. For example, when I observed the chaos in Pam's home and her mother's constant yelling at and criticism of the kids, I understood why Pam acted cranky and quarrelsome in class, and I was able to give her the positive affirmation and love she craved.

FOLLOW-UP

When a student is absent from class, he needs to be contacted by a phone call or note to let him know he was missed and to encourage him to return. If he is absent for several weeks, a visit to his home expresses greater interest and provides an opportunity to discuss the reasons behind the absences.

Regular attenders appreciate some attention too. Phone or write them occasionally to let them know how glad you are that they are faithful in attending class and that you can count on them.

Although junior highers generally receive a number of phone calls, they rarely get mail addressed to them. Keep in touch with everybody by sending notes to say you are thankful they are in your class, to wish them happy birthday, to congratulate them on an accomplishment at school, to compliment them for greater participation in class, to say you are thinking about them, etc.

KEEPING PARENTS INFORMED

In order to enlist cooperation in teaching their junior highers, parents need to be kept informed about what you are teaching and what the class is doing. There are a number of ways of communicating with parents.

Periodic Home Visits

In addition to getting acquainted with students and their families, periodic home visits are excellent times to keep parents informed about studies and their teen's spiritual growth. "This personal contact has been very important to us," one mother commented. "There's no substitute for being informed *personally*."

Parents' Booklet

In connection with visiting in my students' homes, I have used a booklet which describes the current course of study, class-time activities, and ways parents can help. The 5½ x 8½-inch typed or duplicated booklet with construction paper cover is easy to make. See the sample "Parents' Booklet."

Parents' Booklet

(Page 1)

If you are like most parents, the faces on the cover describe you in regards to what goes on in your children's Sunday school classes. Therefore, I would like to introduce you to Belden's junior high girls' class.

Junior highers are such a delightful breed of people—my favorite! They are so open, willing, helpful, and fun to work with. (Yes, that's your daughter I've just described!) Consequently, I really enjoy teaching them.

Please take time to read through this booklet. It will acquaint you with the content of our study, a little of what we do in class, and ways you can help.

(Page 2)

This Quarter's Study

This quarter we are studying the Ten Commandments, focusing on how God's standards apply to us today. In light of the world's view that God's commandments are outdated and unnecessary, our junior highers need to be aware of the facts that God's moral laws never change and that they are just as necessary this year as they were when God originally gave them to the Israelites.

(Pages 3 and 4)

Our Class Time

Class activities vary from Sunday to Sunday. One week we may begin by listening to a song or dialog on a cassette or by taking a quick quiz. We may work out problems with pencils and paper. We may sit in a circle and discuss or break into small study groups.

Sometimes we work on extended projects, such as newspapers, mobiles, banners, or notebooks.

I vary my teaching methods to keep the girls interested, but one thing never changes. Our purpose in meeting is to study the Bible; God's Word is of prime importance. Variety in teaching is only an aid to help interest students in studying it.

I emphasize the practical application of Biblical truth to everyday living. While it is important that our students know what the Bible teaches, it is vital that this knowledge changes their conduct and attitudes.

(Pages 5 and 6)

You Can Help!

I need *your* help in teaching your junior high daughter. Here are some suggestions:

1. See that your daughter is present every Sunday—and on time. If she is sick or will be out of town, I would appreciate a phone call. That way I can be prepared better for class time by adjusting my lesson plans, if necessary, for the number of girls expected.

2. Encourage your junior higher to complete the student

work and learn the memory verse each week. Perhaps a weekly check will be needed to get her in the habit of doing so. This preparation before class helps the girls to be familiar with the lesson topic and better able to participate in class.

3. Discuss the lessons with your daughter—before and after class. Don't be afraid to ask questions about what she is studying. If done on a regular basis, this type of discussion will promote further learning.

4. Be an example. Come to Sunday school and church with your children. We have classes for all ages, including adults.

5. Finally, if you know some way I can help your daughter, please let me know. Also, if you notice changes in attitudes and behavior as a result of what she is studying in Sunday school, I would appreciate knowing. That's the kind of encouragement we teachers need!

As we work together, we both can help your junior higher to "grow in grace, and in the knowledge of our Lord and Saviour Jesus Christ" (2 Peter 3:18).

(Page 7)

If I can be of any help to you or if you have questions about the Sunday school class, please do not hesitate to call me. My phone number is ____________.

Sincerely in Christ,
(Signed)

Name of church
Address
Phone

Quarterly Letters

Another way to keep parents informed is through formal letters. At the beginning of each quarter, duplicate and send a letter describing the new course of study, any special projects your class completed last quarter, approaching activities, and any general class problems. See "Letter to Parents." You may want to add personal notes at the bottom of some or all letters.

One parent told me, "The letters keep us informed about what our children are studying so we can talk about it at home. They rarely tell us themselves."

Letter to Parents

(Date)

Dear Parents:

Next month marks the beginning of a new Sunday school quarter. For the next three months we will be studying a course which deals with the battle between God and His archenemy Satan. We will trace the tactics of Satan from the time he rebelled against God and was cast out of Heaven until his final defeat in the future. Along the way we will compare those tactics to the ones he uses on us today and discover how to defeat him.

Coming up this month is our annual barbecue and photo scavenger hunt. More information will be given in class when we finalize a date.

I'm looking forward to this new quarter with your junior higher.

Sincerely in Christ,
(Signed)

Class Yearbook

A class yearbook meets with instant popularity. Both parents and students look forward to seeing this visual record which can be shown every time you visit in the home. Include pictures of each class member, socials, special projects, birthday and graduation celebrations, and creative study activities in class. The students can arrange and label the pictures in a photograph album. Albums with self-stick pages work well.

Parents have been very enthusiastic about the yearbooks of my classes. As one mother said, "I really enjoy looking at these pictures. I appreciate being able to see what Kim has talked about."

Parents' Open House

Once a year—or more often—invite parents to join your class for the lesson time. This firsthand observation will help them know how you conduct your class better than any report you give them. Be sure to let your students know in advance that the parents have been invited. Make it a special occasion by serving refreshments and displaying class projects.

CLASSROOM

The four walls you label your classroom also can be teachers if they reflect lesson content. Related posters and pictures can enhance or even extend your teaching time. Card shops and bookstores sell posters with Christian themes, especially those from Argus Press. Accent's Junior High curriculum includes at least one poster in each Resource Packet. Or you can make your own, adding one each week for the quarter. During our course on Bible study methods, I made a poster with the definition and directions for each method and posted it after using it to introduce the method.

The bulletin board can teach, too, if you arrange on it cartoons, articles, pictures, and posters related to the quarter's content. A well-stocked file will be a great help!

If the walls of your classroom are concrete, they probably will not hold items taped to them for very long. The best solution I have found is to attach twelve-inch square cork tiles to one or two walls in a horizontal line about nine to twelve inches apart with a special adhesive which can be obtained at building supply or handyman stores (i.e., Sta-Put's Acoustical Adhesive). The tiles become permanently fixed to the concrete and provide lots of space for thumbtacking or stapling visuals. Cork tiles arranged in groups also make great bulletin boards if you do not have one.

Part of utilizing the classroom is keeping it clean and free from accumulated take-home papers and curriculum materials. If necessary, make it a class project to wash or paint (with the trustees' permission) the walls and clean the rest of the room. If you have students with artistic talent, they may want to paint a mural on one wall, again with the trustees' permission. Do what you can with the resources available to make your classroom inviting to junior highers.

Portions of this chapter originally appeared in *Success* (Fall 1980; Fall 1982), and are reprinted here by permission.

QUICK REVIEW

1. A teacher cannot be effective if he does not know the individuals in his class on a personal basis.

T F

2. Home visits provide valuable information about students which could not be known otherwise.

T F

3. Junior highers rarely present discipline problems.
T F

4. Much of the talking and fooling around in class can be ignored rather than being made into an issue.
T F

5. Using the lecture method helps to prevent discipline problems.
T F

6. It is helpful to establish a few rules for the classroom situation and to enforce them.
T F

7. Regular attenders appreciate phone calls and mail as well as absentees.
T F

8. Parents generally know what is being taught in their junior highers' Sunday school class without your telling them.
T F

9. Classrooms themselves are powerful teachers.
T F

Answers:

1. T 2. T 3. F 4. T 5. F 6. T 7. T 8. F 9. T

Appendix

This section contains the following kinds of study helps for using this book as a text for a teacher training class or individual study.

Think About It: If meeting with a group, discuss these questions together. Or write out your answers and compare them with the responses of another junior high teacher.

Study It: These suggestions will guide you to broaden your knowledge of junior highers and teaching techniques through research and observation. Compare your findings with the rest of the group if you are part of a class.

Make It Yours: These projects will help you to practice what you have read. Be prepared to report the results to the training class.

Chapter 1: Welcome to Their World

Think About It

1. Review the list of items at the beginning of the chapter. Which one best depicts a junior higher to you? Why?
2. Think about your own junior high years. What pressures and problems did you have in common with today's young teens? In what ways were the cultural influences different?

Study It

1. Read about adolescence in an encyclopedia and in the introductory chapter(s) of an adolescent psychology book.
2. Skim through several teen magazines to become acquainted with the subjects and advertising.

Make It Yours

Duplicate copies of the following questions (or make up your own) and have your class members answer them anonymously in order to become better acquainted with your students and the pressures with which they are trying to cope.

1. How well could you present the evidences for the creation of man by God and refute evolution?
____ fairly well ____ sort of ____ not at all
2. When you have a problem, who do you usually go to for help?
____ friend ____ parents
____ teacher ____ pastor
3. Have you received helpful advice when you asked for help?
____ yes ____ not enough ____ no
4. How much do you usually watch TV?
____ 1-2 hours per day ____ 3-4 hours per day
____ 5-6 hours per day ____ more
5. What are your three favorite TV shows?
6. What radio station do you listen to the most?
7. What magazines do you read?
8. What types of amusements do you enjoy most?
9. What sports do you participate in?
10. What is the most interesting thing you like to do when you have no other responsibilities?

Chapter 2: Physical Development

Think About It

What was the worst aspect of puberty for you? Why? What was the best part? Why?

Study It

From what you have observed and heard, evaluate where your class members are in their physical development.

Make It Yours

1. Decide which of your students could use some encouragement in relation to their physical development and how you will encourage them.
2. Evaluate the kind of role model you are in relation to a proper attitude toward your body. What changes do you need to make? What steps will you take to improve?
3. Evaluate the amount of involvement and opportunities your students have had to participate in class the past month. What changes do you need to make?
4. If your department does not have separate classes for boys and girls, meet with your superintendent and other teachers to discuss how to implement the change and then follow through.

Chapter 3: Mental Development

Think About It

1. How can you encourage junior highers to use their new thinking ability?
2. What are some ways to respond to students who like to argue?
3. Name some of the do's and don'ts of Christianity which are prevalent in your church. What Biblical principles and standards can you teach junior highers to help them develop their own convictions in these areas?

Study It

1. Read about Piaget's stages of cognitive development in an educational psychology book, concentrating on the last two, concrete operations and formal operations.

2. Review your last four lesson plans to determine how much you involved students and challenged them to use their new thinking ability.
3. Read *Hide or Seek* by James Dobson.

Make It Yours

1. List at least one strength for each of your students plus at least one way you can help him or her develop it further. Then follow through.
2. Plan several ways to build up your students' self-esteem.

Chapter 4: Emotional Development

Think About It

1. What problems do you remember having with your emotions when you were in junior high? How do they compare with the ones your students have?
2. What fears do junior highers have? Why? How do they differ from the ones you had at their age?
3. How can you teach young teens to build their faith on the Bible's teaching, not on their emotions?

Study It

Observe a group of junior highers for an hour or so, and chart their emotional ups and downs.

Make It Yours

1. Duplicate copies of the statements in the section entitled "Lack of Self-Esteem," and have your students complete them.
2. Ask your students what fears they have. Decide how you can help them overcome those fears.

Chapter 5: Social Development

Think It Over

1. How can you help both students and their parents as junior highers struggle for more independence?

2. How can you help each class member feel that he is an important part of the group?

3. Do you think junior highers should be discouraged from dressing like their friends, talking like them, etc.? Why or why not?

Study It

1. Find out what heroes your students currently are idolizing.

2. Observe your students around church. Who talks with whom? Who sit together in the church services?

Make it Yours

1. Make a chart of the social groupings in your class. Determine how to form small study groups to cut across cliques without separating everyone from all of his or her close friends.

2. Plan—with your class—a group service project to help your students practice their Christianity.

3. Evaluate the example you are to your students. What would they learn about Christianity if they observed you for a week? What changes do you need to make? List steps to take in the next few weeks to become a better role model.

Chapter 6: Moral Development

Think About It

1. How can you help junior highers relate Biblical truths to the problems they are facing?

2. Do you agree with the saying, "He who has never doubted has never really believed"? Why or why not?

3. What doubts have you had about God, the Bible, Christianity? How did you work through them?

4. What specific things can you do and say to encourage junior highers to make spiritual decisions without manipulating them or playing on their emotions?

Study It

1. Watch some of the television shows and listen to some of the music your students enjoy to determine the kinds of values which are influencing theirs.

2. Read a book or two on apologetics so you will be prepared to answer your students' questions and doubts about Christianity.

Make It Yours

1. Find ways for junior highers to serve at church and channel them into those opportunities.

2. Plan ways to help students understand the value of personal Bible study and Scripture memorization.

Chapter 7: You, the Teacher

Think About It

1. Who is the most memorable teacher in your life, either positively or negatively? Tell or list three reasons why you remember him or her as outstanding. Was he a Sunday school teacher?

2. How does a teacher's spiritual life affect his teaching?

3. What opportunities are available for you to increase your Bible knowledge and to develop your teaching skills?

4. In what specific ways can you show love to junior highers?

Study It

Read about communication and/or counseling skills, especially concentrating on developing good listening skills.

Make It Yours

1. Review the list of ways to discover the gift of teaching. Evaluate yourself with this list, including consultation with others.
2. Evaluate your personal preparation as a teacher. Identify areas in which you can improve and specific ways to do so.
3. List specific ways to affirm students in the next few weeks.

Chapter 8: Principles of Teaching and Learning

Think About It

1. When you read the two different teaching situations at the beginning of the chapter, which class did you think was learning the most? Why? In what ways did the chapter change or confirm your ideas?
2. Define teaching and learning in your own words.
3. How can a teacher cooperate with and depend on the Holy Spirit as he prepares and teaches?

Study It

1. Read 1 Corinthians 2:1—4:5. List God's part and our part in serving the Lord.
2. Using a concordance, study what the New Testament says about the Holy Spirit's ministry in our lives, relating the truths discovered to a teaching ministry.

Make It Yours

Review your last three or four lesson plans. How do they measure up to the eight principles of teaching and learning in the chapter? In what areas do you need to improve? Choose one, and list steps to take in the next few weeks.

Chapter 9: Lesson Preparation

Think About It

1. Choose a lesson in your teacher's manual. What adaptations do you need to make in order to meet the needs of your students?
2. How can evaluation be a welcome word?

Study It

1. Visit a Christian bookstore, your church library, or your pastor's library to look at reference books.
2. Decide which resource books you would like to own as a beginning of your personal library or an addition to your present collection of study books.

Make It Yours

1. Start a teaching file, using the guidelines in the chapter.
2. Study the Bible passage for your next lesson by using the three steps given under "Procedure."
3. Prepare your next lesson plan by using the guidelines in the section entitled "Lesson Plan."
4. Take the self-evaluation test in the chapter.

Chapter 10: Teaching Methods

Think About It

1. What factors should you consider when deciding if the methods in your teacher's manual are appropriate for your students?
2. Choose a lesson in your teacher's manual, and decide if

the suggested methods are appropriate for your class. If not, what changes need to be made?

3. What specific responses can you give when a student answers a question incorrectly?

Study It

Observe other teachers using some of the methods described in the chapter.

Make It Yours

1. Practice writing good questions, using the guidelines in the chapter.

2. Practice using the methods in this chapter whenever they are suggested in the teacher's manual or are appropriate for your aims and content.

Chapter 11
Aids to Better Teaching

Think About It

1. Read Mark 6:30-44. What audio-visuals could you use to help teach this passage? How could writing a news story and conducting an interview help your students learn more from this passage?

2. How could you involve your students in the preparation and use of transparencies for the overhead projector?

Study It

1. Study a Sunday newspaper. List all of the features which could be used in a Bible newspaper.

2. Watch several game shows on television, and determine which ones can be adapted for Sunday school reviews and how.

3. Browse in stores which sell games. Choose several which can be adapted for reviewing Bible content and application.

Make It Yours

1. Plan a review game for the end of your next quarter of study.
2. Use several new audio-visuals in your next few teaching sessions.

Chapter 12: Inside and Outside the Classroom

Think About It

1. What do you want to know about your students so you can teach them more effectively?
2. What discipline problems do you have with junior highers? How do you handle them? How can you improve your classroom management?

Study It

1. Study your classroom carefully; then list everything that needs to be done to improve it. Begin to follow through.
2. Visit several card shops and bookstores. Browse through the posters for ones you can use in your teaching.

Make It Yours

1. Use the personal interview questions and the "Let's Get Acquainted" form to get to know your students better.
2. Schedule visits to each of your students' homes.
3. Begin a class yearbook.
4. Plan a class social.
5. In the next few weeks, send a note to all the students in your class.

Bibliography

Barnes, Jonathan, *The Complete Works of Aristotle*, vol. 2. Princeton, NJ: Princeton University Press, 1984.

Butler, Trent. "To Doubt Is To Learn." *Youth Leadership*, April-June, 1985, pp. 20, 21.

Carroll, Lewis. *Alice's Adventures in Wonderland*. Garden City, NY: Children's Classics, n.d.

Dobson, James. *Hide or Seek*, rev. ed. Old Tappan, NJ: Fleming H. Revell, 1974.

Doan, Eleanor L. *431 Quotes from the notes of Henrietta C. Mears*. Glendale, CA: Regal Books, 1970.

Elder, Carl A. *Youth and Values: Getting Self Together*. Nashville: Broadman Press, 1978.

Fischer, Kurt W.; Lazerson, Arlyne. *Human Development*. New York: W. H. Freeman and Company, 1984.

Frame, Randy. "Child Abuse: The Church's Best Kept Secret?" *Christianity Today*, February 15, 1985, pp. 32-34.

Inhelder, B.; J. Piaget. *The Growth of Logical Thinking*, New York: Basic Books, 1958.

Lasch, Christopher. *The Culture of Narcissism*. New York: W. W. Norton & Company, Inc., 1979.

McCasland, Dave. *From Swamp to Solid Ground*. Wheaton, IL: Victor Books, 1980.

Naisbitt, John. *Megatrends*. New York: Warner Books, 1984.

Pippert, Rebecca Manley. *Out of the Salt-Shaker & into the World*. Downers Grove, IL: InterVarsity Press, 1979.

Rice, Wayne. *Junior High Ministry*. Grand Rapids, MI: Zondervan Publishing House, 1978.

Search Institute. *Young Adolescents and Their Parents*, Summary of Findings. Minneapolis, MN: Search Institute, 1984.

"The Unheard Cry," *Success*.

Toffler, Alvin. *Future Shock*. New York: Random House, 1970.

Towns, Elmer L. *Successful Biblical Youth Work*. Nashville: Impact Books, 1973.

"When 'Family' Will Have a New Definition," *U.S. News and World Report*, May 9, 1983, pp. A3, A4.

Index